T0003314

The New York Times

CLASSIC CROSSWORD PUZZLES
100 Puzzles

Edited by Will Shortz

ST. MARTIN'S GRIFFIN   NEW YORK

First published in the United States by St. Martin's Griffin,
an imprint of St. Martin's Publishing Group

THE NEW YORK TIMES CLASSIC CROSSWORD PUZZLES.
Copyright © 2020 by The New York Times Company. All rights reserved.
Printed in China. For information, address
St. Martin's Publishing , 120 Broadway, New York, NY 10271.

www.stmartins.com

All of the puzzles that appear in this work were originally published
in *The New York Times* from January 22, 2018, to October 2, 2018;
or from January 2, 2019, to August 10, 2019.
Copyright © 2018, 2019 by The New York Times Company.
All rights reserved. Reprinted by permission.

ISBN 978-1-250-62354-6

Our books may be purchased in bulk for promotional, educational, or business use.
Please contact your local bookseller or the Macmillan Corporate and Premium
Sales Department at 1-800-221-7945, extension 5442, or by email at
MacmillanSpecialMarkets@macmillan.com.

First Edition: 2020

10   9   8   7   6   5

DIFFICULTY KEY

Easy:

Medium:

Hard:

1

ACROSS
1 Ponzi schemes, e.g.
6 Agatha Christie or Maggie Smith
10 Times past noon, informally
14 "Sounds exciting . . ."
15 Iranian currency
16 Applaud
17 Cutting-edge brand?
18 2016 Best Actress Oscar winner for "La La Land"
20 Unwelcome looks
22 Somewhat
23 Encouragement for a matador
24 Half of a half step in music
26 Relieved (of)
27 Biden and Pence, informally
28 Abbr. in an office address
29 Pacific source of unusual weather
31 Stoic politician of ancient Rome
33 Places to get quick cash
36 Chess endings
37 Weight unit equal to about 2,205 pounds
40 Group of eight
43 Gym locker emanation
44 On the briny
48 "Legally ___" (Reese Witherspoon film)
50 Fix, as an election
52 Be nosy
53 "Leaving ___ Vegas"
54 "Puh-LEEZE!"
58 Like the name "Robin Banks" for a criminal
59 Make, as money
60 Grand stories
61 Enthusiastic audience response, informally
64 Bit of clowning around
66 Title of a list of errands
67 ___ Wallace, co-founder of Reader's Digest
68 Fish typically split before cooking
69 Sudden problem in a plan
70 Look for
71 Ariana Grande's fan base, mostly

DOWN
1 "Red" or "White" baseball team
2 Deep-fried Mexican dish
3 Div. for the N.F.L.'s Jets
4 Less talkative
5 Laughs through the nose
6 "Forgot About ___" (2000 rap hit)
7 Put in the cross hairs
8 Caribbean ballroom dance
9 "Seinfeld" character who wrote for the J. Peterman catalog
10 One of two in "Hamilton"
11 Go from 0 to 60, say
12 What sunning in a swimsuit leaves
13 Racer's swimwear
19 Sailor's patron
21 Start to attack
24 Home shopping inits.
25 Back in style
30 Grandmother, affectionately
32 Muscat is its capital
34 Prefix with life or wife
35 Look down on
38 Swirled
39 Jiffy
40 Administrative regions in Russia
41 Eric who sang "Layla"
42 Deep-fried Mexican dish
45 Bond film after "Skyfall"
46 Natural process illustrated by the last words of 18-, 24-, 37-, 54- and 61-Across
47 Novelist Rand
49 Inbox buildup
51 Exceed
55 "Sesame Street" character long rumored to be Bert's lover

by Paolo Pasco

56 Something acute or obtuse

57 Chop finely

62 Holiday drink

63 Tree with acorns

65 Successors to LPs

2 ★

ACROSS

1 Value of snake eyes in craps
4 Rules as a monarch
10 Difficult endeavor
14 Put on TV
15 87, 89 or 93, on a gas pump
16 With 25-Down, office request
17 Pro at tax time
18 In any place
20 Counterparts of compressions, in physics
22 Wear away
23 ___-X
24 "Get serious!"
25 Member of a Marvel Comics group
29 Divinity school subj.
30 T-X connection
33 Neighbor of the asteroid belt
34 Strip discussed in the Oslo Accords
36 Word with circle or ear
38 Nobel laureate Wiesel
39 Opinion pieces
41 Nashville venue, informally
42 Mork's TV pal
44 Wait for a green light, say
45 Fire and fury
46 Peculiar
47 It doesn't get returned
49 Less sincere, as a promise
51 Make black, in a way
52 El Al hub city
53 "Already?"
56 City straddling Europe and Asia
61 Foreboding
63 Judge Lance of the O.J. trial
64 Book after Chronicles
65 Surface
66 Grazing area
67 Drakes : ducks :: ___ : swans
68 Apt word to follow each row of circled letters
69 Subtext of Jefferson Airplane's "White Rabbit"

DOWN

1 Diplomat's skill
2 Film editor's gradual transition
3 Leftover in a juicer
4 Olympic sport with strokes
5 Repeat
6 Calif.-to-Fla. route
7 Elongated, heavily armored fish
8 U-turn from SSW
9 Opening word?
10 Rear admiral's rear
11 ___ flow
12 Green-lit
13 Richard of "Unfaithful"
19 Coins of ancient Athens
21 Picked up on
24 Place to sing "Rock-a-Bye Baby"
25 See 16-Across
26 Bona fide
27 A narcissist has a big one
28 Relative of an épée
30 Concern for a debt collector
31 Brink
32 More sardonic
35 End of a line on the Underground?
37 Antivirus software brand
40 Divinity sch.
43 Logo with an exclamation mark
48 Annual French film festival site
50 Smoothed out
51 Deep sleeps
53 Particular in a design
54 Ricelike pasta
55 Belgrade denizen

by Jim Hilger

56 Anatomical canal
57 Royal title
58 Outfit in Caesar's senate
59 Pac-12 team
60 Mutual fund consideration
62 Little rascal

3

ACROSS

1 Scuttlebutt
7 ___ Fridays (restaurant chain)
10 Slob's creation
14 Hedy in Hollywood
15 Dessert topper from a can
17 And others, in a bibliography
18 Estrange
19 Org. for Penguins and Ducks
20 Wintry coating
22 Vice president Spiro
23 Cunning
25 Spill the beans
28 Online source for health info
30 Take a stab at
34 "Ye olde" place to browse
36 Up to, as a particular time
37 Govern
38 Goopy roofing material
39 High U.S. Navy rank
42 Farrow in films
43 Building annexes
45 Particle with a charge
46 Thief
48 Students' simulation of global diplomacy, informally
50 Arctic abode
51 "Scram!"
53 Sleepover attire, informally
55 Twisty curves
58 The "P" of PRNDL
60 Scanned lines on a pkg.
62 Diminish the work force . . . or a literal hint to the answers to the four starred clues
65 Deficiency in red blood cells
67 Ship-related
68 Searched thoroughly, with "through"
69 Fighting force
70 Raises
71 Praises highly

DOWN

1 "Galveston" singer Campbell
2 Inauguration Day vows
3 *"Crazy to run into you here!"
4 Erie Canal mule of song
5 Blue or hazel eye part
6 *Newspapers or magazines
7 Fish with a heavy net
8 Form of some shampoo
9 Amin exiled from Uganda
10 One circulating at a party
11 "Trainspotting" actor McGregor
12 Building lot
13 Spurt forcefully
16 Gave a hand
21 Brit. resource for writers
24 "You betcha!"
26 Den
27 *Contest for an areawide seat
29 Controversial chemical in plastics, for short
31 *Nonsense
32 Ballerina's bend
33 Drop running down the cheek
34 Pipe part
35 Angel's band of light
36 Sardine container
40 Like early LPs
41 Response to an online joke
44 Age reached by a septuagenarian
47 1940s–'50s jazz
49 Asian yogurt drink
50 "This ___ test"
52 German cars with a lightning bolt logo
54 Long-winded sales pitch
55 Poet ___ St. Vincent Millay
56 Rise quickly
57 Taken a dip
59 U.S. fort with very tight security

by Lynn Lempel

61 Scoundrels
63 Post-O.R. area
64 Stick in the microwave

66 Fire dept. responder, maybe

4 ⭐

ACROSS

1 Sun Devils' sch.
4 Like the Llwynywermod royal estate
9 One free carry-on bag, for many domestic flights
14 Large body of eau
15 Welcome on Waikiki
16 Light-footed
17 Collar
18 Japanese soup tidbit
20 "Frozen" snowman
22 Like the lion's share
23 Pavarotti, for one
25 Part of a barn where hay is stored
26 Ones approving fin. statements
30 Hot and arid
33 Iota preceder
34 Wisconsin city that's home to Lawrence University
36 Coco of couture
37 ___ Spiegel (German newsmagazine)
38 Piglet producer
39 Something to shoot for
40 Hip-hop artist with the #1 album "Hip Hop Is Dead"
41 Study, with "on"
43 Large Greek olive
45 Actor Cary of "The Princess Bride"
46 Dictionary
47 Bombard
48 Red Sox archrival, on scoreboards
49 Jazzy James and Jones
52 Historically significant
56 Land celebrated on March 17
57 Like most pet dogs . . . or a hint to this puzzle's circled letters
61 Big fuss
62 Evicts
63 O'Connor's successor on the Supreme Court
64 Company V.I.P.
65 Extract forcefully
66 Title for un hombre
67 Medium power?

DOWN

1 Juvenile retort
2 Bobby who co-founded the Black Panthers
3 Growing problem in cities?
4 "___ is hell"
5 Israeli carrier
6 ___ Linda, Calif.
7 General who said the quote at 4-Down
8 "Not so fast!"
9 Vientiane's country
10 "Ha! You fell for my trick!"
11 Central
12 Feeling down
13 Simple top
19 Unfamiliar
21 Stable newborn
24 Monkey often used in research
27 Subject of some September sports reporting
28 Irritated no end
29 Lively Latin dance
31 Riding, say
32 Ticket info
33 Ancient Balkan region
34 "Mad Men" type, informally
35 "Get Out" director Jordan
36 City WSW of Bogotá
39 Opposite of bellum
42 Hates
43 Peeper's vantage point
44 Speck
46 Stretchy materials
48 San Francisco's ___ Hill
50 West Wing workers
51 Poke around
53 Annoyance
54 Similar (to)

by Emily Carroll

55 Jared who won an Oscar for "Dallas Buyers Club"

57 Word after show or know

58 Sharer's word

59 "It's no ___!"

60 Neither's partner

5

ACROSS

1 Possesses
4 Grape-Nuts or Apple Jacks
10 Ewe's offspring
14 Man's name that's an investment spelled backward
15 Pumpkin color
16 Revered one
17 Pot's cover
18 Traditional night for partying
20 Side of a diamond
22 Thomas ___, "Rule, Britannia" composer
23 Bowling target
24 Texas landmark to "remember"
27 Sampled
29 Curved Pillsbury item
33 Misplace
34 "The Way We ___"
35 "Yeah, right!"
39 Pie ___ mode
40 Detectives
42 Batman portrayer Kilmer
43 Deserve
45 ___-Pacific (geopolitical region)
46 Something to click online
47 Ones calling the plays
50 Teeter-totter
53 Walk with a swagger
54 Every last drop
55 Parade spoiler
58 "Piece of cake" or "easy as pie"
61 40-hour-a-week work
65 Guadalajara gold
66 Actress Falco of "Nurse Jackie"
67 "Hot" Mexican dish
68 Prefix with natal or classical
69 Clarinet or sax
70 Crossed home plate, say
71 One who might follow into a family business

DOWN

1 50%
2 Song for a diva
3 Early TV comic known for "Your Show of Shows"
4 Popular cold and flu medicine
5 "But I heard him exclaim, ___ he drove out of sight . . ."
6 Uncooked
7 One-named Irish singer
8 Ending with golden or teen
9 Makeshift shelter
10 Fleur-de-___
11 Highly capable
12 Multiplex offering
13 Mix
19 Kingdoms
21 "Anything ___?"
25 Whimper like a baby
26 Like most Bluetooth headsets
28 Underhanded
29 Tight-lipped sort
30 Part to play
31 Be confident in
32 Fixes, as shoelaces
36 Forcible removals, as of tenants
37 Pull hard
38 Civic-minded group
40 Fictional mouse ___ Little
41 Male deer
44 Mensa stats
46 Lavish praise on
48 Hangs around for
49 Gave some money under the table
50 More secure
51 Give the slip
52 Actress Kemper of "Unbreakable Kimmy Schmidt"
56 Apple on a desk
57 Pixar's "Finding ___"
59 Nabisco snack since 1912

by Alan Arbesfeld

60 It has phases that are represented by the starts of 18-, 29-, 47- and 61-Across . . . and by 1-Down

62 Was in front

63 Pickle holder

64 Bullfight cheer

ACROSS

1 Loud commotion
4 Yeshiva leader
9 Films on a grand scale
14 Year, in Spain
15 If a > b and b > c, then a > c, e.g.
16 Kind of lily
17 Winter solstice mo.
18 Lowest point for Americans?
20 Crow
22 Like nylon stockings
23 Audi rival
24 Like the architecture of many cathedrals
27 Visibly blushing
29 American-made sports car with a V-10 engine
32 Plains Indian
33 Posted announcement at a theater entrance
34 Andean capital

35 Southernmost of the Ivies
36 Bass, e.g.
40 Storage tower
43 Mount that has an insurance company named after it
44 Commotion
47 Solvers' cries
48 Film character who says "Give yourself to the dark side"
51 Poll worker's request
53 From the beginning: Lat.
54 Prefix with center
55 Nosy sort
58 ___ room (postdebate area)
59 Prototype, maybe
63 Item in Santa's bag
64 Exhaust
65 Dim with tears
66 Closemouthed
67 Blog entries
68 More or less, informally
69 Letter before tee

DOWN

1 Some schlumpy male physiques
2 Mistakenly
3 "Sorry, Charlie!"
4 Wicked cool
5 Dismiss abruptly
6 Favoritism
7 Not just one or the other
8 Arriver's cry
9 Online greeting
10 Bud
11 "O.K., tell me more"
12 The Tigers of the A.C.C.
13 Pourer's instruction
19 Zig or zag
21 [This tastes awful!]
25 Prefix with commute
26 ___ Wilcox, daughter in E. M. Forster's "Howards End"
28 Amazing, in slang
30 Rapscallion
31 Road worker

36 Rx detail
37 Mel who was the first N.L.'er to hit 500 home runs
38 How many TV shows are shown nowadays
39 Give in
40 Put some money away
41 "Fingers crossed!"
42 SoCal daily
44 Sign on a real or virtual pet
45 Tricky . . . or a tricky description of 18-, 29-, 36-, 48- and 59-Across
46 Words and phrases that sound approximately alike, like "ice cream" and "I scream"
48 Eat stylishly
49 Cute, in modern slang
50 Reply to a ques.
52 Replies to an invitation

by Bruce Haight

56 ___ Accords (1990s peace agreements)
57 Common fishing spot
60 Openly gay
61 ___ bran
62 Org. that sticks to its guns?

ACROSS

1 Horror sequel of 2005
6 Reverberation
10 Movers' vehicles
14 Sow, as seeds
15 Clammy
16 Theater award
17 Best-selling autobiography by Priscilla Presley
19 Be the best, in slang
20 Michelle of the L.P.G.A.
21 Any singer of the 1973 #1 hit "Love Train"
22 Actor John of "Problem Child"
24 Neil who sang "Laughter in the Rain"
26 Antiriot spray
27 State capital ESE of Guadalajara
33 Like a porcupine
36 Woods nymph
37 Cartoon "devil," informally
38 Window part
39 Sanders in the Pro Football Hall of Fame
40 Jazzman Stan
41 Onetime competitor of the WB
42 Machine near the end of a car wash
43 ___ Island (amusement park site)
44 Many a 1970s remix
47 Rock's Clapton or Burdon
48 Dressed for a classic fraternity party
52 Fixes, as a photocopier
55 Front's opposite
57 Sch. in Charlottesville
58 Dove calls
59 One with credit . . . or a literal hint to 17-, 27- and 44-Across
62 Queue
63 What separates Nevada from Colorado
64 Barely visible, as a star
65 Rarely getting rain
66 Hang in the balance
67 ___ the bill (pays for something)

DOWN

1 Shoots out
2 "Kate & ___" of 1980s TV
3 Signaled with the hand
4 Singer Kamoze with the 1994 hit "Here Comes the Hotstepper"
5 "There, there"
6 Author Ferber
7 Suffragist Elizabeth ___ Stanton
8 "Lemme think . . ."
9 1990s "Saturday Night Live" character with a cape
10 Whirlpool
11 Touch
12 Stream near the Great Pyramids
13 Crystal ball user
18 Cleanser brand with a name from mythology
23 Like some sprains and tea
25 Primo
26 City hall V.I.P.s
28 High muckety-muck on Madison Avenue
29 Town ___ (colonial figure)
30 Major Calif.-to-Fla. route
31 Oscar-winning actress Blanchett
32 Rocker Osbourne
33 Tater
34 Big ___ (longtime Red Sox nickname)
35 B&Bs
39 Tennis tournament since 1900
40 Percussion in a Buddhist temple
42 Wriggler on a fishhook
43 "Iron Chef" competition

by Michael Black

45 Brought to a halt
46 Poison ivy symptom
49 Sound part of a broadcast
50 Happening
51 Pub game
52 Home of the N.C.A.'s Bruins
53 Pinot ___
54 Folk singer Mitchell
55 Muffin material
56 What Ritalin helps treat, for short
60 Had a bite
61 "7 Faces of Dr. ___" (1964 film)

8

ACROSS

1 Unwanted email
5 Series of courses?
10 "Buenos días!"
14 Actress Polo
15 Top Trappist, maybe
16 14-time M.L.B. All-Star, to fans
17 Beginning, datewise
18 "Yes, that's my opinion"
20 Like skim milk
22 Takes to the station house
23 Wolf (down)
26 One-named singer with the 2016 #1 hit "Cheap Thrills"
27 The "O" of NATO: Abbr.
30 Physics Nobelist Bohr
32 Big rift
36 Intrinsically
38 Lived like a single guy
40 The "E" of Q.E.D.
41 With 44-Across, Valentine's Day gift . . . or a hint to the shaded squares
42 Regarding
43 The Eternal City
44 See 41-Across
45 Knocks
46 Old school
48 North Africa's __ Mountains
49 On the down-low
50 Looks to be
52 When to expect someone, for short
53 Airer of "The Bachelor" and "The Catch"
55 Stonehenge priest
57 Dakota tribe that attacked "The Revenant" trappers
61 Enthusiastic
65 Get fouled up, idiomatically
68 Manual reader
69 Father of Phobos
70 Snicker sound
71 "Encore!"
72 Some hard drinks
73 Does some post-shooting film work
74 Reason for a school closing

DOWN

1 Baseball's Musial
2 100 centavos
3 Elvis's middle name
4 Irks
5 Tiki bar drink
6 Flow out
7 Fiver
8 The "her" in the lyric "I met her in a club down in old Soho"
9 Excites
10 Try some Valentine's Day candy?
11 Shipments to smelteries
12 Heading on a poster with a picture of a dog
13 Hubbubs
19 Philosopher Fromm
21 Fashion's Klein
24 PC start-overs
25 Big source of omega-3 fatty acids
27 Schedule at the Met
28 Keep going in Yahtzee
29 One of 22 for U2
31 Pilot
33 Commercial success?
34 Poker advice for Sajak?
35 Greek peak, briefly
37 Try some Valentine's Day candy, sneakily?
39 Investments with fixed rates, for short
41 Item under a blouse
47 "Oops, sorry!"
48 Locale of both the 2018 and 2020 Olympics
51 Bags for guys
54 Home of King Minos
56 Bongos, e.g.
57 Lab medium
58 Actor Calhoun
59 "Hmm . . ."
60 Bedazzled

by Bruce Haight

62 Has the stage
63 Famed "fiddler"
64 Sprouted

66 Sushi fish
67 "Nevertheless
. . ."

9

ACROSS

1 Skirt bottoms
5 Ticklish Muppet
9 Gets thin on top
14 With: Fr.
15 Banquet
16 Lewis and ___ Expedition
17 GARFIELD + U = Beach V.I.P.
19 "___ at the Bat"
20 City NW of Detroit
21 "Help me, Obi-Wan Kenobi," e.g.
23 Home for Nixon and Reagan: Abbr.
24 "It's a date!"
26 MADISON + A = "Me, too!"
29 Shakespearean cries
30 Bounding main
32 Pathetic group
33 Mysterious sighting in the Himalayas
35 Some rulings on PolitiFact
38 Mortgage, e.g.
39 FILLMORE + V = Movie buff

42 Like racehorses' feet
44 Who asks "What can I help you with?" on an iPhone
45 Author Silverstein
49 Soccer blocker
51 President pro ___
53 Lab eggs
54 HARDING + P = Squeezable exercise tool
57 Actor Snipes of "White Men Can't Jump"
59 Approves
60 Famous ___ cookies
62 River of Cologne
63 Uncle Sam's land, for short
66 COOLIDGE + P = Narc's four-footed helper
68 Humdingers
69 Panache
70 Pistol sound
71 Hybrid picnic utensil
72 Philosophies
73 First half of a Senate vote

DOWN

1 Two-year mark, in a presidential term
2 Wicked look
3 Egoistic demand
4 National Mall, for a presidential inauguration
5 Six-foot bird
6 ___ years (when presidents are elected)
7 Maples formerly married to Donald Trump
8 Like the days of yore
9 Send covertly, as an email
10 Leader in a state roll call: Abbr.
11 Milan opera house
12 "You wish!"
13 Like atria
18 Onetime Pontiac muscle cars
22 What a majority of campaign spending goes toward

25 Dickens's Little ___
27 Store sign on Presidents' Day
28 Aromas
31 Gets ready to shoot
34 "Too rich for my blood"
36 QB Manning
37 Separate, as whites from colors
40 "Got it!," beatnik-style
41 ABC show on weekday mornings, with "The"
42 Absorbs
43 "Star Wars" pilot
46 There's one to honor presidents every February
47 The slightest amount
48 What hens do
49 Grave robbers
50 Word after many presidents' names
52 Bygone Ford make, briefly
55 Celebrated Chinese-born architect

by Bruce Haight

56 Diving venues
58 Queen of ___ (visitor of King Solomon, in the Bible)
61 Poetry competition
64 Mink or sable
65 Query
67 Political connections

ACROSS

1 Something sticking out of Frankenstein's neck
5 Voting coalition
9 Belittle
14 Classic Langston Hughes poem
15 "__ Land" (2016 Best Picture nominee)
16 French author who said "An intellectual is someone whose mind watches itself"
17 Alabama senator Jones
18 Home to Zion National Park
19 Walk with heavy steps
20 adj. under the influence of a drug
23 Long, boring task
24 __-blogging
25 adv. across a barrier or intervening space
30 Singer DiFranco
31 Smoked salmon
32 Bonus
34 "Can I get a hand here?!"
36 Like William Henry Harrison, among U.S. presidents
39 Crowd favorite not getting nominated for an Oscar, e.g.
40 Cough drop brand
42 Apply carelessly, as paint
44 Fresh __ daisy
45 n. spirit, animation
49 Heading with check boxes below it
50 Main part of a selfie
51 Ones who produced the clues for 20-, 25- and 45-Across
57 Sports center
58 Big name in in-flight internet
59 "About __" (2002 movie)
61 Enliven
62 Midmonth date
63 Target of splicing
64 Emails that tell you you've won the lottery, e.g.
65 Fit one inside the other
66 Energy units

DOWN

1 Creation of an Olympic city hopeful
2 "Then again . . . ," in texts
3 Birthplace of Muhammad Ali
4 Switch between windows, e.g.
5 Beat badly
6 Behind schedule
7 "Frozen" snowman
8 U.S. marshal role for John Wayne
9 Brand of probiotic yogurt
10 Makes the rounds?
11 Mine: Fr.
12 Battle of the bulges?
13 FS1 competitor
21 Sound that signifies the end of a basketball game
22 Actress Vardalos
25 When "S.N.L." ends on the East Coast
26 Louis __, French king who was guillotined
27 Consumer giant that makes Bounty, for short
28 "Cimarron" novelist
29 Extinguish
30 "That hits the spot!"
33 LeBron James's org.
35 Credit card designation
37 Confucian path
38 Popular left-leaning news site
41 Nestlé candy popular at movie houses
43 Humdrum
46 Veiled oath?

by Joel Fagliano

47 Bean
48 Mammoth time period
51 Delays
52 Viking explorer
53 "Hercules" spinoff
54 Went by motorcycle, say
55 Census data
56 iTunes download
60 "Suh-weet!"

11

ACROSS

1 Big name in banking
6 Tempest
11 Something to download
14 "The Fox and the Grapes" author
15 Ancient Asia Minor region
16 Subject for "Dunkirk" or "Apocalypse Now"
17 Defenseless target
19 Hawaii's Mauna ___
20 Pitching stat
21 Transmits
22 Hall-of-Fame Broncos QB John
24 Artsy Big Apple neighborhood
25 "Crazy Rich ___" (hit 2018 movie)
26 Directive that's in force until canceled
31 Eagles' nests
32 Puerto ___
33 Just a touch
36 Lobbying org. for seniors
37 Pioneer in email
38 Wild's opposite
39 "'Sup, ___?"
40 New Age energy field
42 Part of an urn that can turn
44 Notice when getting fired
47 Scarf down
49 Big parts of donkeys
50 Birds that honk
51 Justice Sotomayor
53 Furry foot
56 Meadow
57 Repeated comical reference
60 Like most things in "Ripley's Believe It or Not!"
61 Words said just before dinner
62 Stan's buddy of old comedies
63 Pre-C.I.A. spy org.
64 "Holy cow! This could be bad!"
65 With ___ in sight

DOWN

1 Lawyer's assignment
2 Prince, to a throne
3 "The Thin Man" dog
4 One in need of drying out
5 Unit of a TV series
6 Agree to join
7 Newsman Chuck
8 Burden
9 Ocasek of the Cars
10 Muddles through with what one has
11 Middle school years, notably
12 Song of praise
13 Says "Dear God . . ."
18 Sodas not much seen nowadays
23 It can be white or boldfaced
24 Small scissor cut
25 Path of a Hail Mary pass
26 Bygone Swedish auto
27 Bit of weeping
28 Images on Kansas City Chiefs' helmets
29 A pun can induce one
30 Resource extracted from Alaska's North Slope
34 Roman god of love
35 Wagers
37 NPR's Shapiro
38 Much of a salon worker's income
40 Peanut or pollen reaction, possibly
41 Hawaiian instrument, for short
42 Land on the Strait of Gibraltar
43 Model of excellence
45 Small batteries
46 Ones who are said to grant three wishes
47 Eskimo home
48 Must-haves
51 Crackle and Pop's buddy

by Trent H. Evans

52 Fairy tale beginning
53 Tree : Christmas :: ___ : Festivus
54 Similar (to)
55 Dandelion, for one
58 Spoon-bending Geller
59 Singer and former "American Idol" judge, familiarly

12

ACROSS

1 "Gotta go!"
6 Reject, as a lover
11 Snub-nosed dog
14 ___ panel (rooftop installation)
15 Retouch a base after a fly-out
16 Wall St. debut
17 In unison
19 Sternward
20 Vote in favor
21 "Right now!," to a surgeon
22 Hoity-toity sort
23 The idea that matter is composed of small, distinct components
27 Unfailingly
30 Respond to a stimulus
31 Secure, as a ship
32 Just the way you see me
34 Actress Thurman
37 Common taxi destination
41 Show with many notable alums
42 Oozes
43 Late playwright Simon
44 ___ Lama
46 Without bias
48 Big department store in a mall, e.g.
52 Pepsi, e.g.
53 Word spoken before and after "James"
54 Star athlete, for short
57 Network showing "Suits" and "Mr. Robot"
58 When Pac-Man and Rubik's Cube were popular . . . or a phonetic hint for 17-, 23-, 37- and 48-Across
62 "Whether ___ nobler . . ."
63 Department store that once famously put out catalogs
64 Pop music's Hall & ___
65 Hesitant speech sounds
66 Rockne of Notre Dame fame
67 Seize forcibly

DOWN

1 Words before "old chap"
2 Double agent
3 Earthen pot
4 Chubby
5 Snowman of song who's "a jolly, happy soul"
6 Sauna sight
7 Musical Page
8 "Yecch!"
9 Lament
10 "Morning Edition" airer
11 One involved with a grand opening?
12 Enthused about
13 Coped, barely
18 Sporty Pontiacs of old
22 Mo
23 Seniors' org.
24 Gets emotional at a wedding, maybe
25 Sheds a ___ (24-Down)
26 Soccer star Mia
27 You love: Lat.
28 Beef cut
29 Top-of-the-line
32 Wiped out, as while skateboarding
33 Nascar additive
35 A lot of it is junk
36 Italy, to Germany, in W.W. II
38 Capital due north of the northern tip of Denmark
39 Keister
40 "What's ___ for me?"
45 "Now I see!"
46 Vampire's telltale sign
47 "You can say that again!"
48 Severe but short, as an illness
49 Polite refusal
50 Film critic Roger
51 Racket

by Bruce Haight

54 Smidgen
55 Pair of skivvies?
56 [Over here!]
58 "You should know better!"
59 One laying an egg
60 __ Claire, Wis.
61 Paving goo

13

ACROSS

1 Sticker that says who you are
6 Part of the body that crunches work
9 Dreadlocks wearer, informally
14 The "F" of R.A.F.
15 Kitten's sound
16 Use as a dinner table
17 Zero-tariff policy
19 Back's opposite
20 Shaggy grazer
21 Orders (around)
23 Swanky
24 Beginning blossoms
25 With 39-Down, last words in many an old movie
27 Six-sided game piece
28 With 45-Across, savory topping found in tubs . . . and the circled squares?

31 Complete lack of wind, as at sea
33 Feeling good to wear, say
34 Languages
35 Iced tea brand in a bottle
36 When repeated, gets specific, as an informer
37 "Where there's ___, there's hope"
40 Guinness world record holder for longest live weather report
42 Alternative to an S.U.V.
43 "Cat on a Hot Tin Roof" actor
45 See 28-Across
46 Pen filler
47 ExxonMobil product
48 Work's opposite
49 Bowled over
51 Messiah
53 Only three-letter zodiac sign
56 "Well, obviously!"

58 Device to remove water from a ship
60 Aged fairy tale character
61 "We're number ___!"
62 Worth
63 Secondary building
64 Marry
65 Wide-mouthed jugs

DOWN

1 Far from certain
2 ___ the Explorer
3 Journey
4 Crackerjack
5 "Start working!"
6 Accumulate
7 Where flowers and oysters grow
8 Sugar, e.g.
9 Wearer of stripes on a court, informally
10 Grp. making after-work plans?
11 Moved out of the way

12 Throat part
13 "O Canada," for Canada
18 Was a passenger
22 Retrieves, as baseballs
24 Happened to
26 Last part of U.R.I.'s URL
28 Includes in an email
29 Slangy ending for "any"
30 Began, as a voyage
31 Mosque toppers
32 Waldorf salad ingredient
34 Acknowledges applause, maybe
36 Bursting stars
38 Org. overseeing airports
39 See 25-Across
41 Oil ___ (gulf sight)
42 "Oh, puh-leeze!"
43 Human rights advocate Jagger
44 Like brand-new clothing

by Jacob Stulberg

45 Trudge
48 Stacked
50 Sand ridge
52 Grape or watermelon plant
53 Item in a tackle box
54 Mideast bigwig
55 Chooses, with "for"
57 Bit of voodoo
59 Where parishioners sit

ACROSS

1 Information about other information
9 Make harmless, as a snake
15 "Original copy" or "open secret"
16 "Ma-a-aybe"
17 Shy sort
19 Broke ground?
20 "You ___ busted!"
21 Ambulances' hosp. destinations
22 Epithet for a British beauty with fair skin
28 Magnificent
30 Grp. meeting in a school gym, often
31 Long in the tooth
32 "Buffalo Bill," for William Cody
34 Warm and cozy
35 High-flown speech or writing . . . or a description of 17-, 22-, 51- and 57-Across?
41 Chops (off)
42 Poseidon's realm
43 Letters on a wanted poster
44 $ource of ca$h
47 Places in one's cross hairs
51 Try to improve what is already beautiful
54 Meadow
55 Very heavy
56 Flying nuisance
57 Full of energy and enthusiasm
63 1996 best-selling guide for "grammar-phobes"
64 One registering with the American Kennel Club
65 Chooses for office
66 Gumbo cookers

DOWN

1 Dances violently
2 Urge strongly
3 Rapper/actor Gibson
4 In the thick of
5 High-ranking Mafioso
6 "Raiders of the Lost ___"
7 You, to Yves
8 Record of a year's events
9 Dump, as stocks
10 Elevator innovator Otis
11 Stop on an elevator
12 "Talking" system for the deaf, in brief
13 Born, in high society
14 Comprehend
18 Firm hold
22 Fashion magazine with a French name
23 Hair removal brand
24 Color of an overcast sky
25 Actress Chaplin of "Game of Thrones"
26 Counterfeit token
27 Rim
29 Legislatures write them
33 ___-mo replay
34 Like arias and anthems
35 Something planted when claiming territory
36 Troublemaking Norse god
37 Milky white gem
38 Opening on Broadway?
39 Onetime radio host Boortz
40 Larson who created "The Far Side"
44 If everything goes right
45 Grad student's big paper
46 Blend well together
48 Pacific current that causes odd weather
49 Cups, saucers, sugar bowl, etc.
50 Lustful goat-men of myth
52 Kind of column in ancient Greece
53 Things detectives pursue
56 Stare slack-jawed

by Timothy Polin

57 Slack-jawed feeling
58 Note after fa
59 Broker's charge
60 Boozehound
61 Grow long in the tooth
62 ___ Jones industrial average

ACROSS

1 Shoot out, as 14-Across
5 Peach stones
9 Demanding that people do this and do that
14 Volcanic rock
15 Uncork, as a bottle
16 Livid
17 At the lower side of the pH scale
18 Maple or oak
19 Stepping on the baseline when serving in tennis, e.g.
20 Holder of wires along a street
23 Gloom's partner
24 Actor Efron of "The Greatest Showman"
25 Subway scurrier
28 Like one end of a battery: Abbr.
31 Aggressive defensive soccer maneuver
34 Midterm or final
36 That, in Tijuana
37 Eco-conscious Dr. Seuss character
38 Red facial spots
39 Transmits
42 Toward sunrise
43 ___-wip (dessert topping)
45 "Black gold"
46 Nickname for John Wayne, with "the"
47 Series of funny outtakes
51 Smidgen
52 Fashion designer's monogram
53 Have another birthday
54 Golf ball props
56 Toy in a 2017 craze
62 Cricket's sound
64 Pairs
65 College in New Rochelle, N.Y.
66 Pavarotti, voicewise
67 Inner: Prefix
68 Some natural hairdos, for short
69 Horned safari animal
70 Student body overseer
71 Use the items found at the ends of the answers to 20-, 31-, 47- and 56-Across

DOWN

1 Part of a bed's base
2 Tempo
3 Wicked
4 Walked through water
5 Things filled by a highway crew
6 "On my honor!"
7 Adolescent
8 Something that's impossible to do with one's eyes open, per an urban legend
9 Dual-purpose bit of eyewear
10 Of the mouth
11 Hot dog topper
12 The Cards, on a scoreboard
13 Up until now
21 Like one end of a battery: Abbr.
22 Consoling touch
26 Anchorage's home
27 Communicated via iMessage or WhatsApp
28 In the area
29 Gets all A's, say
30 James ___, portrayer of Tony Soprano on "The Sopranos"
32 Benefactor
33 Like mixed doubles tennis, in college
35 "Love ___" (Beatles hit)
40 Fizzy, sugarless beverage
41 Takes a night to think over
44 Apple tablet with an attachable keyboard
48 Omelet or quiche ingredient
49 Like clarinets and oboes
50 Hawaiian garland

by Caitlin Reid

55 Quick smell
57 Hotel amenity with a cord
58 Adjust, as a piano
59 "Me neither"
60 Grandson of Adam and Eve
61 What talcum powder may prevent
62 Middle: Abbr.
63 The laugh of someone who's up to no good

16

ACROSS

1 Shout to a pest
5 European capital whose name most people incorrectly accent on the second syllable
10 Actress ___ Pinkett Smith
14 N.B.A. coach Steve
15 Drenched
16 Road sign with an arrow
17 Chromebook competitor
18 How a hamburger may be ordered
20 Flammable gas represented in 18-Across and 9-Down
22 Dance in the days of doo-wop
23 Unwelcome acknowledgment
24 Wearers of kilts
29 What "*" may mean in a reference book
32 "!!!"
33 Ambulance driver, for short
35 "Bye for now!"
36 1990s BP acquisition
38 Respiratory gas represented in 36-Across
41 Back tooth
42 Part of da-DUM, da-DUM, da-DUM
43 ___ soap
44 Santa ___ winds
45 Where the lowest-numbered avenues in Manhattan are
48 Clothing brand with a horse head logo
50 Devices that may serve as cash registers
54 Like non-Rx meds
55 Pungent-smelling gas represented in 57-Across and 49-Down
57 "Sixteen Candles" director, 1984
62 "It's urgent" in the E.R.
63 "No way, José"
64 Bandmate of Harrison, Lennon and McCartney
65 "S.N.L." alum Fey
66 Kind of dancer
67 Bar, in legalese
68 Do a price check on, e.g.

DOWN

1 Removes, as cream
2 Charles Atlas and others
3 Speak to a crowd
4 Group in a pit
5 Cut, as logs
6 Day care knee scrape, e.g.
7 Beef marbling
8 "Sorta" suffix
9 Sneeze sound
10 Vehicles made for rough terrain
11 Word after fire . . . or a synonym of fire
12 Put down, in slang
13 "No thanks, I already ___"
19 Means of hair removal
21 "Come as you ___"
24 Fixed time
25 Insurance filings
26 Easily changing emotions
27 One leading the festivities
28 CARE, e.g., in brief
30 W.W. II arena
31 Send into exile
33 Low-cost prefix
34 Of the cheek
37 Distance markers along a highway
39 ___ mints
40 Kimono sash
41 Rank under Lt. Col.
46 Blame, as for a crime
47 Like 10-watt light bulbs
49 "Tiny Bubbles" singer
51 Very silly
52 1981 royal bride
53 The Devil
55 Flying start?

by Greg Johnson

56 Letters on an auto sticker
57 Earthenware container
58 "Well, what have we here?!"
59 Clasp
60 Sporty autos
61 Protection against sunburn

17 ⭐

ACROSS

1 Just one year, for Venus and Serena Williams
7 Small plumbing problem
11 ___-Caps (candy)
14 It gets beaten at a party
15 McEntire with a twang in her voice
16 Long, long time
17 Remove, as from a belt
18 Popular program usually shown back to back with 34-/36-Across
20 Strong brews
22 Speaker's place
23 Host of 18-Across
27 One of four on a fork
28 Anger
29 Some hospital pics
30 Ham and lamb
31 Immigrant's class, for short
32 Money that may go in a slot
33 Purchase at Citgo
34 With 36-Across, popular program usually shown back to back with 18-Across
36 See 34-Across
40 Engine cooler
41 Lose vibrancy, as from exposure to sunlight
42 H.S. proficiency exam
43 Vegas hot spot, with "the"
46 One-liner
47 Smelting refuse
48 Uzbekistan and Kazakhstan's ___ Sea
49 Co-host of 34-/36-Across
51 "You can stop explaining the joke to us"
53 Peter, Paul and Mary, e.g.
54 Co-host of 34-/36-Across
56 Notices
60 "Who am ___ say?"
61 Actress ___ Flynn Boyle
62 Kathmandu native
63 Cookbook amt.
64 "___ Eyes" (Eagles hit)
65 It shakes things up

DOWN

1 Kwik-E-Mart clerk on "The Simpsons"
2 Alcohol that's transparent
3 Accompanier of a letter inside an env.
4 Samsung product
5 At an angle
6 Movie for which Tatum O'Neal won an Oscar
7 Nickname for Erving in the old N.B.A.
8 ___ Pieces
9 Onetime Apple product
10 One of the Three Bears
11 Country below Hungary
12 "Stop, I beg you!"
13 Banded gems
19 Precollege exam that offers college credit
21 Sans ___ (font type)
23 Not many
24 Like green, green vegetation
25 Writer ___ Stanley Gardner
26 Big storage item
30 Mother with a foal
32 Applaud
33 Aunt or uncle, sometimes
35 Does one's taxes online
36 Like light from a far-off star
37 Unattractive fruit
38 "Awesome!"
39 Perimeter
41 "Ain't we got ___?"
43 Ditch for cutting timber
44 Pays for everyone
45 Convertible, in slang
46 From Doha, e.g.
47 Quaint store
49 Golfer Singh who won the 2000 Masters

by Michael Black

50 More sagacious
52 Always bumping one's head on doorways, say
55 Topeka's home: Abbr.
57 "Are you?" response
58 "Strange Magic" band, in brief
59 Ma'am's counterpart

18 ★

ACROSS

1 Secondhand
5 Native of Muscat
10 Drama units
14 Like photos that violate one of Instagram's community guidelines
15 Betray by selling out
16 Unadorned
17 Legendary N.Y.C. punk rock club
18 Really vex
19 Common picnic side dish
20 Leave gobsmacked
21 W.W.E. head Vince ___
23 By way of
24 Verbally consented
26 Coming to
28 Tenor Ronan ___
29 Early hrs.
32 Something "common" that's not really so common
33 Like bats, cats and rats
36 With 40-Across, comment to someone who 30-Down
39 Amanda of Nickelodeon's "The Amanda Show"
40 See 36-Across
44 "Great" primate
45 Church recesses
46 "Selma" director DuVernay
47 Courage
50 Antonym: Abbr.
51 Hit a four-bagger
53 To the point that
54 ___ of Good Feelings
55 Absolutely love
56 Network on the telly, with "the"
57 Cool, to a jive talker
58 Go a mile a minute
59 Pulitzer-winning playwright for "Both Your Houses"
63 "___ you serious?"
64 Eurasian animals with antlers
65 Before, to poets
66 Donkey
67 Foot bones
68 Wet blanket?

DOWN

1 Still to be filled, as a role
2 With 12-Down, places where a thoughtless person 30-Down
3 Enter by sidling
4 Ball belle, briefly
5 Hoover competitor
6 "Just the facts, ___"
7 Lead-in to girl or boy
8 Biblical patriarch-turned-sailor
9 Being pulled
10 Muscles in sit-ups, informally
11 Comics boy who says "Reality continues to ruin my life"
12 See 2-Down
13 Underground waste
21 "___ Lisa"
22 Org. prominent at Cape Canaveral
25 Title for Judi Dench
27 Casino game
29 "Parks and Recreation" star
30 Crowds one's seatmates, in a way . . . or a hint to the circled letters
31 Nighttime breathing disorder
34 Deg. for a C.E.O.
35 Magazine no.
36 Four-time N.B.A. champ Ginobili
37 Free drink locales
38 Corners in geometry
41 Skedaddled
42 Always, quaintly
43 Like a steak that's "still mooing"
48 Panorama, e.g.

by Ross Trudeau

49 Mount ___, highest peak in the Rockies

51 Abusive sorts in a fraternity

52 Scent

59 Goat's call

60 Hawaii's Mauna ___

61 Joe Biden's state: Abbr.

62 Never-before-seen

ACROSS

1 West Coast law force, for short
5 Insurer whose name rhymes with "quack"
10 Q-tip, e.g.
14 Regions
16 Where the Dolphins play
17 Prey for cats
18 Characters in a play, formally
21 Unit of corn
22 Loopy from drugs
23 Some herding dogs
24 Monarch renowned for his wealth
28 N.Y.C. subway inits.
29 Down Under hoppers, informally
30 Overlook rudely
33 Ice cream treat
36 Veer, as a ship
37 Miracle-___ (garden brand)
38 With 39-Across, doomsayer's assertion . . . or a phonetic hint to 18-, 24-, 51- and 61-Across
39 See 38-Across
42 Santa ___ winds
43 "How stupid of me!"
46 More tidy
47 Trail mix
49 Japanese noodle
50 61, in old Rome
51 College team from the land of Lincoln
57 How TV series DVDs may be sold
59 DNA sequence
60 Gen ___ (millennial forerunner)
61 Yom Kippur War clash
65 Response from a greatly amused texter
66 Better aligned
67 Goes way, way up
68 Bellow
69 Comic Bruce with a foul mouth
70 Big Board inits.

DOWN

1 Stows, as cargo
2 Pianist Claudio
3 Gem strung on a necklace
4 Beaver's construction
5 Mexican friend
6 Popular Friday feast
7 Once around the track
8 Soul: Fr.
9 Ringling Brothers offering, once
10 Round-the-campfire treats
11 Going off script
12 Smoothie "superfruit"
13 "Subjects" of a queen, not a king
15 Like the climate of the African desert
19 Like some auto windows
20 "Like father, like ___"
25 Beach washer
26 Breath-taking snake
27 Specification on an airline ticket
31 Desire
32 Physics Nobelist Niels
33 Without a date
34 "You might think so, but . . ."
35 Grave, as injuries
39 Queued
40 Strictly platonic
41 Hammer's target
43 Bit of an ellipsis
44 Japanese sash
45 Do a surfing maneuver
48 Glock, for one
49 Jewish village of old
52 Dr. Scholl's padding
53 Architect Frank
54 No, in pig Latin
55 Comes closer
56 "And Still ___" (Angelou volume)
57 With competence

by Chuck Deodene

58 Uncreative bar order, with "the"

62 Metal before refinement

63 When said three times, a Beach Boys hit

64 Charged particle

20 ★

ACROSS

1 Mends with stitches
6 Schools of thought
10 Glasgow girl
14 Heavenly hunter
15 Process part
16 John Irving's "A Prayer for ___ Meany"
17 Megacorporation? [1996, 1970]
19 Singer Suzanne
20 Sorrowful sound
21 Exception to a "no pets" policy
23 Prison sentence
25 N's in Athens
26 Pomade? [1968, 1972]
32 Where G.I.s fought in the '60s
35 Stitch loosely
36 Like some pitchers

37 Milan's La ___
39 Worthless amount
40 Lifted
41 Electrical unit
42 Tech support callers
44 Dapper fellow
45 Supreme Court that's corrupt? [2003, 1982]
47 Swelled head
48 Language that gave us "boondocks"
54 Rectify
59 Render harmless
60 Cab competitor
61 Melted? [2018, 2012]
63 Voice on a phone
64 Annapolis inst.
65 Roman wraps
66 To be, to Bizet
67 It's sold in bars
68 Cubic meter

DOWN

1 ___ Ferry, N.Y.
2 Running wild
3 Severity
4 Night, in Nogales
5 Elitist sort
6 AOL, e.g.
7 Deer sir?
8 Carte that comes before the course
9 Secret agent's activity
10 Parlor piece
11 Immensely impressed
12 Utah's state flower
13 Fly in the ointment
18 Shade of brown
22 A shotgun wedding might be held under this
24 Doesn't take things too seriously
27 Formal response at the door

28 University official
29 Star Yankees 3B for 10 seasons
30 Ward of "The Fugitive"
31 Fall setting
32 Office-inappropriate, in web shorthand
33 ___ na tigela (fruity Brazilian dish)
34 Artist Chagall
35 Ne'er-do-well
38 War of 1812 locale
43 Duane ___ (pharmacy)
46 Dork
49 Folksy restroom sign
50 In progress
51 Fencing move
52 Hollywood honor
53 V-formation fliers
54 Artist's inspiration

by Paul Coulter

55 Not much

56 Deborah who starred in "The King and I"

57 Guesstimate phrase

58 Lady of Spain

62 Stick in the microwave

ACROSS

1 ___ San Lucas (Baja resort city)
5 Chew the fat
8 Maze runner in an experiment
14 Brewery products
15 Pitcher's stat
16 "Uncle!"
17 Five-time N.B.A. championship-winning coach with the Lakers and the Heat
19 Cable channel with many science shows, familiarly
20 "Ready, ___, fire!"
21 Ballad, e.g.
23 Circus enclosure
24 Garfield, to Jon Arbuckle
27 Notable statistic for Jeff Bezos or Bill Gates
29 Opening number?
30 Prosciutto, e.g.
32 Physicians, for short

33 Obtain
34 Mountain overlooking Tokyo
37 Casino floor V.I.P.
40 Make tiny criticisms
43 Ruler of old Russia
44 Broadcast
45 ___ tai (cocktail)
46 Bygone monthly for the 12-to-20 set
50 "The A-Team" actor with a mohawk
51 Road hazards that need filling
54 "Be patient!"
56 "Your turn," on a walkie-talkie
57 Appear to be
59 Surface of a sty
60 Peeved
62 Dessert loaf
66 Cheap cigar, slangily
67 CBS forensics franchise
68 Midwife's delivery
69 Sailor

70 "I know what you're thinking" feeling, for short
71 First word in a fairy tale

DOWN

1 Salary limit
2 ___ carte
3 Software trial runs
4 Duel overseer in "Hamlet"
5 Do stuff?
6 Warlike Greek god
7 Musket attachment
8 Width's counterpart
9 Santa ___ winds
10 Proceeding from low to high
11 America's largest firearm manufacturer
12 Secret ___ (007, for one)
13 Egyptian god usually pictured with the head of an ibis
18 Apple computer

22 Neighbor of Homer on "The Simpsons"
24 "___ and Circumstance"
25 Break off a relationship
26 Yanks (on)
28 Drift, as an aroma
31 Hi-___ screen
35 Singer with the 1961 hit "Big Bad John"
36 Comforting words
38 Place to shower and brush one's teeth
39 Cookie with creme in the middle
40 Never, in Nuremberg
41 Tehran's land
42 Eartha who sang "C'est Si Bon"
44 Perfect attendance spoiler
47 Yankees legend ___ Howard
48 Originally named
49 Egyptian pyramid, e.g.

by Andrew Kingsley

51 John, Paul and John Paul
52 Undeveloped seed
53 Four: Prefix

55 High-performance engine
58 Dishevel, as the hair

61 Work ___ sweat
63 Extra 15% or so for a waiter
64 Simple as ___
65 Henna, for one

ACROSS

1 Baker's dozen?
5 Wild feline
11 Path of the tip of a pendulum
14 Lacking vegetation
15 Marie ___ (women's magazine)
16 "Gloria in excelsis ___" (carol chorus)
17 *Starting point, metaphorically
19 Equivalent of "Inc." in the U.K.
20 7'6" N.B.A. star ___ Ming
21 Gossip
22 Outrage
23 Michael of "Batman" and "Birdman"
26 *Important part of a plane
28 Longtime weatherman of morning TV
30 Eastern "way"
31 Where a fishing boat ties up
32 Tidy
35 Fathers, as foals
39 Stars-and-stripes land
40 *A swimsuit might leave one
42 Electronica producer Brian
43 Sample
45 Cry made while taking a bow
46 Dame ___ Everage
47 Good rating for a bond
49 Ties, as a score
51 *Powerful object in "The Hobbit"
56 Baghdad residents
57 King Kong, for one
58 Old Palm smartphone
59 Critical hosp. wing
60 Low-I.Q.
61 What may be created using the answers to the six starred clues?
66 Musical Yoko
67 Played on the green
68 Mythological figure who takes a bow
69 Noted number on Downing Street
70 Parts of college applications
71 Like the part of a pool with a diving board

DOWN

1 Recede gradually
2 With 51-Down, star of "Wonder Woman"
3 *Ill-defined situations
4 Long-term legislator
5 Abbr. in an email field
6 Portuguese greeting
7 Cozy accommodations for a traveler, informally
8 Counterpart of criminal
9 Where Noah's Ark landed
10 Precedent setter in court
11 Off-script remark
12 Nostalgia-evoking, as fashion
13 Ancient handwritten volume
18 Loony
23 Done for
24 Form of Elizabeth
25 "99 Luftballons" singer
27 Pond carp
29 Landlord's income
33 Doug Jones's home: Abbr.
34 Best-selling detergent brand
36 *Moscow landmark
37 Ho-hum feeling
38 Detergents, e.g.
40 Opening strip on a package
41 Blue race in "Avatar"
44 Small bit
46 Passed, as laws
48 Boeing rival
50 Rock's Burdon or Clapton
51 See 2-Down
52 Offer a thought
53 Clunker of a car

by Freddie Cheng

54 Digs made of twigs
55 "__ go!"
62 Heroine of "The Force Awakens"
63 YouTube revenue source
64 Fish spawn
65 Seasoning amt.

ACROSS

1 Become narrower
6 "Come to __"
10 Kindergarten fundamentals
14 "Well, isn't that something!"
15 Genesis garden
16 Opening for a coin
17 Facial feature that can be eliminated by cosmetic surgery
19 Trigonometric ratio
20 "For sure!"
21 "__ put it another way . . ."
22 Rather, informally
23 Disney World attraction
26 Walk over
29 Continuously
30 Easy win
31 __ good example
32 Weaponize
35 Increase, with "up"
36 Friend of Archie and Betty in the comics
39 "Little piggy"
40 Chum
41 Fashion monthly founded in France
42 Congers and others
43 "__ ed Euridice" (Gluck opera)
45 The 20 in 20 Questions
48 Speak briefly
51 Where the belly button is
52 German auto import
53 Try to win through romance
56 Metro-politan __
57 "Gross" title for this puzzle
60 Hit the tarmac, e.g.
61 Skin problem
62 Titleholder
63 This, in Tijuana
64 Wagers
65 Hangman's loop

DOWN

1 Having everything in its place
2 Natural salve
3 Asset
4 Flow out, as the tide
5 Insert a new cartridge
6 Marmalade ingredient
7 For one purpose only
8 Architect I. M. __
9 Actress Miller or Blyth
10 Transfer (to)
11 Romantic setups
12 Weeklong vacation rental, maybe
13 Prepare, as mussels
18 Therefore
22 Work, as dough
23 It helps to know where you're going
24 Joint between the hip and ankle
25 Letter after theta
26 Snare
27 Capital of Italia
28 Professional work
31 "Steady as __ goes"
33 Part in a movie
34 Filthy state
36 "The Family Circus" boy
37 Peter Fonda title character
38 Give off light, as a firefly
42 Suffix with lion or shepherd
44 Marriott rival
45 Seriously overcharges
46 Pakistani language
47 Incandescent lamp inventor
48 Old, as bread
49 Surrounding lights

by Craig Stowe

50 "There __ a dry eye in the house"

53 Tippler's favorite radio station?

54 Bills exchanged for a five

55 Menacing fairy tale figure

57 Tiny amount to apply

58 Rink surface

59 A couple

ACROSS

1 Object of puppy love
6 Acid's opposite
10 Eponymous scale inventor
14 Skating gold medalist Sonja
15 Big farm workers
16 Country whose name can also be a full sentence
17 Welcome comment at a bar #1
19 Lead-in to bank
20 "Ooh, ooh, let me look!"
21 Cornered, as during a fox hunt
22 Milky birthstone
23 Welcome comment at a bar #2
27 Actor George of TV's "The Goldbergs"
29 Underhanded sort
30 Some univ. instructors
31 Friend of Harry in the Harry Potter books
33 The Cardinals, on scoreboards
34 "Hang on!"
35 Welcome comment at a bar #3
39 "This is not ___" (warning to kids)
40 Cleverly and ironically humorous
41 Tina Fey's "30 Rock" role
42 ___-1701 (U.S.S. Enterprise registry)
43 Often-forbidden things to worship
45 Caesar's first stabber
49 With 57-Across, welcome comment at a bar #4
52 Sounds of support
53 Cousins of mandolins
54 Pestering people
56 Words before "smoke" or "the air"
57 See 49-Across
60 Dirt ball
61 One coming to homecoming, maybe
62 "The Burning Giraffe" and "The Persistence of Memory"
63 Boy dolls
64 "Beg pardon!"
65 They might make lids difficult to close

DOWN

1 Women's clothing chain since 1983
2 Do again, as a radio bit
3 Let off the hook?
4 Likewise
5 Casual greetings
6 Termites and drills
7 Pink-slip
8 Maritime milieu
9 Tolkien tree being
10 Tiny opening?
11 Avenue between Reading Railroad and Chance
12 Poison-pen letters
13 Most sarcastic
18 ___ Talks
21 "Shame!"
24 Fashionable
25 Home of The Hague: Abbr.
26 Superman's birth name
28 Wood in a fireplace
32 Change of locks?
34 Pointed headgear often pictured with stars and moons
35 Tabloid twosome
36 Manner of speaking
37 1982 film inspired by Pong
38 Big lighter brand
39 "Were you successful at all?"
43 Some digital chats, informally
44 Holy councils
46 How Solomon spoke

by Samuel A. Donaldson

47 French sweetheart

48 Make a judgment of

50 Rips to pieces

51 The Great Lakes' ___ Locks

55 3:2 or 10:1, e.g.

57 Independent charity, for short

58 Spanish gold

59 Clothing chain since 1969

ACROSS

1 Turkish bigwig
6 Norway's capital
10 Luke, to Darth Vader ("Star Wars" spoiler)
13 Released from bondage
14 Bounce, as off a billiard cushion
15 Israeli gun
16 Regal
18 Bellum's opposite
19 "___ Te Ching"
20 Brother of Cain
21 Nothing more than
22 Yosemite and Yellowstone
27 Mike who was a three-time N.L. M.V.P. with the Phillies
29 Close
30 Big piles
31 Make a quick drawing of
35 Address in a browser, for short
36 What a bald tire lacks
38 Ending with neutr- or Filip-
39 "The View," for one
42 Flower in a pond
44 Finished, as a cake
45 Heading on a personal bio
47 Something promised in a court oath
51 Hot-rod engine, informally
52 Love, in Latin
53 Prefix with friendly
56 "A Nightmare on ___ Street"
57 Cause championed by the figures named at the ends of 16-, 22- and 47-Across
61 Travel on Alaska or Hawaiian
62 ___ Beckham Jr., three-time Pro Bowler for the New York Giants
63 Pageant crown
64 Many Ph.D. candidates
65 Fish trying to find Nemo in "Finding Nemo"
66 In a foxy way

DOWN

1 Dismissive sound
2 Opera solo
3 Roman Catholic-affiliated university in New Jersey
4 Playboy founder, for short
5 Ruckus
6 Like bourbon barrels
7 Country once known as Ceylon
8 Actor Chaney of "The Phantom of the Opera"
9 Texter's "Holy cow!"
10 "Terrific!"
11 Missouri's ___ Mountains
12 Puts the kibosh on
14 Early North American explorer John
17 Bug spray from S. C. Johnson
21 Podcaster Maron
23 Box on a concert stage
24 "___ the season . . ."
25 Green building certification, for short
26 Bit of butter
27 Close
28 Actor Michael of "Juno"
31 Stitch
32 Go to bed, informally
33 "E pluribus ___"
34 Prepare for a photo
36 One of the Huxtable kids on 1980s–'90s TV
37 Australian winner of 11 Grand Slam tournaments
40 Native New Zealander
41 U.S.C. or U.C.L.A.: Abbr.
42 Funny Costello
43 Openly gay
45 Island with a lagoon
46 "It's c-c-cold!"
47 Pilferage
48 Very, slangily
49 More than 60 awards for "Saturday Night Live"

by Sean Biggins

50 One of the Brontë sisters

54 ___-Alt-Del

55 Start of "The Star-Spangled Banner"

57 Fish caught off the New England coast

58 Wedding affirmation

59 Word before "a bird," "a plane" and "Superman!"

60 Baseball's Hodges

ACROSS

1 Jan. honoree
6 Mild reprimands
10 Industrial vessels
14 "Old MacDonald" refrain
15 State said to be "high in the middle"
16 "Thus with a kiss ___" (Romeo's last words)
17 Glider measurement
19 "Have you ___ wondered . . . ?"
20 Close calls
21 Certain close-knit social media group
22 "Brigadoon" co-star Charisse
25 Actor Wilson who has appeared with Ben Stiller in 12 films
26 Maker of the Pathfinder and Rogue
27 Grilled order with corned beef
29 Accomplished
30 Before, in poetry
31 Long past time?
32 Guinness record holder for the U.S. city with the most consecutive days of sun (768), informally
35 "Look out!" . . . and warning when encountering the circled things in this puzzle
40 "Fingers crossed!"
41 Baseball's Matty, Felipe or Moisés
43 Some people have a gift for it
46 Wall St. starter
47 Addressee modifier on an envelope
49 Media sales team, informally
51 Auto company since 1899
53 Org. for Jaguars, but not Panthers
54 Big blows
55 Idiot
57 French military hat
58 Massive electoral victories
62 The "E" of Q.E.D.
63 Biblical twin
64 Creepy looks
65 M&M's that were discontinued from 1976 to 1987 over fears about their dye
66 Chip's cartoon partner
67 Rear admiral's rear

DOWN

1 Kitten's call
2 Super Bowl of 2018
3 Burns in film
4 Lively dances
5 ___ Lee Browne, actor/director in the Theater Hall of Fame
6 Yankee Joe whose #6 was retired
7 Glossy look
8 Hyundai alternatives
9 Lawn order
10 YouTube popularity metric
11 Counsel
12 Accessory for a cravat
13 Peaceful
18 Places where goods are sometimes fenced
21 Listings in a nautical table
22 Shout
23 "Dang, that hurts!"
24 ___ mater (brain membrane)
26 Hobbyists' racers controlled remotely
28 Transaction with a bookie
29 ___ ex machina
33 Ore, for one?
34 "The Cask of Amontillado" writer
36 Contents of a poker pot
37 Damage, as a reputation
38 Zeno of ___ (philosopher)
39 [And it's gone!]
42 Mixed martial arts org.
43 Rubbernecker

by John E. Bennett and Jeff Chen

44 Stick (to)
45 Bikini insert
48 Ring-shaped islands
50 Sends out

51 What follows the semis
52 "It should be my turn soon"

55 Org. behind the New Horizons probe
56 Nutritionist's plan

58 Was in front
59 Ruby of the silver screen
60 Blunder
61 Nine-digit ID

ACROSS

1 Joint that a sock covers
6 Small recess
11 Karl Marx's "__ Kapital"
14 Country star Tucker
15 Theater worker
16 Month with Columbus Day: Abbr.
17 Giving away unwanted items rather than trashing them
19 Second letter after epsilon
20 Rage
21 Luau dance
22 Absorbs, as gravy on a plate
24 Broccoli __
26 Clark of the Daily Planet
28 Obsessive to a fault
29 The Supremes' "__! In the Name of Love"
30 Extra job in the gig economy
33 Gin's partner in a classic drink
35 Look at, in the Bible
36 Put in more ammunition
39 Greeting in Tel Aviv
42 Lessens, as pain
44 Alternatives to Nikes
46 Dramatically end a speech, in a way
51 Result of a traffic ticket
52 Many, many, many, many, many moons
53 Hanker (for)
54 Ex-senator Bayh
55 "Hold your horses"
58 Tear to bits
60 Mind's I?
61 Reaction to an overshare
62 Crowdfunding site . . . or a hint to the beginnings of 17-, 30- and 46-Across
65 Goal
66 Inventor Howe
67 Prefix between tri- and penta-
68 Martial arts master Bruce
69 What a star on the American flag represents
70 Slightly off

DOWN

1 Initially
2 Holden Caulfield, for "The Catcher in the Rye"
3 Patella
4 Chemical compound with the formula NaOH
5 Made for __ other
6 Centers of atoms
7 Components of archipelagoes
8 Second letter after upsilon
9 Roosters' mates
10 Therefore
11 "Crime __ pay"
12 Real
13 Alternative to a paper clip
18 Hardy-har-hars
23 Previous incarnation
25 Disorder resulting in seizures
27 Bagful carried by a caddie
31 When repeated, a sneaky laugh
32 Mil. branch with B-52s
34 Paint layer
37 Wood for a baseball bat
38 Profound
40 Classic typewriter brand
41 Bosses
43 Look smugly upon
45 Madrid matrons
46 Insurance type that often accompanies medical
47 Dormmate, e.g.
48 Punctual
49 Existing: Lat.

by Thomas van Geel

50 Coin with Lincoln on it
56 Barely makes, with "out"
57 Pinball fail
59 Facts and figures
63 Spying org.
64 Band with the 1993 hit "Everybody Hurts"

28

ACROSS

1 Barred from competition, briefly
5 Prefix with economics
10 Sportsbook offering
14 Liqueur with a licoricelike flavor
15 Psychologist Alfred
16 Stumble around in a daze
17 Empty talk not backed by action
19 Screenwriter James of "The African Queen"
20 Santa ___, Calif.
21 Slender
22 Play loudly, as music
23 Like all natural numbers: Abbr.
24 Boost after appearing on a certain old Comedy Central show
27 Malia Obama's sister
29 Use an oar

30 Lion in the heavens
31 In effect
35 Arkin of "Catch-22"
36 Product from RCA or LG
39 Something traced to draw a turkey
40 Get, as from a will
41 "___ the least I can do"
42 Groceries holder
43 Sedan alternative
47 Symbol of the completion of the Transcontinental Railroad
52 Upper extreme, informally
53 Stockpile
54 Work without ___
55 Gift for which you might reply "Mahalo"
56 Happening now, as a telecast
57 Sport hinted at by the ends of 17-, 24-, 36- and 47-Across

60 Universal donor type, for short
61 Paragon
62 Christmastime
63 Exchanges "I do's"
64 Sounds from a pet owner's lap
65 Column on a flight board, for short

DOWN

1 Practice swimming
2 Trendy food from the Andes
3 Toll method on the New Jersey Turnpike
4 Uno + uno
5 Kingpin on "The Wire"
6 Excedrin competitor
7 Do some mountaineering
8 DVR button
9 Molybdenite, for molybdenum
10 Toothpaste brand
11 Airport named for a president
12 Venison

13 Take some time to consider
18 Break free
22 Texter's segue
25 Orange Muppet
26 Whirler on a whirlybird
28 "Please ___" (secretary's words)
32 Water with the Alps in its logo
33 Men's gymnastics event
34 Bit of volcanic fallout
35 Apropos of
36 Luke Skywalker's home planet
37 Forced into bondage
38 Fine point
39 Poker variant in which the worst set of cards splits the pot
42 The first "B" of B&B
44 German mark
45 Spanish rice dish
46 Banishees
48 Bottom of the barrel

by Benjamin Kramer

49 Primitive kind of diet

50 Holiday guest that a couple might fight over

51 Starting points in shipbuilding

57 Get-up-and-go

58 Payment of tribute?

59 "Ciao!"

29

ACROSS

1 Two of a kind
5 Buildings near barns
10 Stinging insect
14 Bone alongside the radius
15 Jack in a deck of cards
16 Camera setting for amateur photographers
17 Paranoiac's headgear
19 Walked (on)
20 Up, in baseball
21 Straps for an equestrian
22 Soak (up)
25 Present en masse
28 Pen pal's plea
30 Like a Monday crossword, typically
31 Actress Chlumsky of "Veep"
32 Part of the eye
33 In the past
36 "This means trouble, my friend"
41 Motor oil product
42 Hero fighter pilots
43 Partner of "go seek"
44 Celebrity
45 Keeps under surveillance
48 Blueberries and fatty fish, nutritionists say
51 Visitors from outer space, for short
52 Without toppings
53 Walled city WNW of Madrid
55 Watermelon waste
56 Dirt . . . or what 17-, 25-, 36- and 48-Across all have?
61 Gives a tattoo to
62 ___ and true
63 Not spicy
64 Soup to go with sushi
65 Delicious
66 Potato, informally

DOWN

1 "___ 'er there!"
2 "The Greatest" boxer
3 Lodging for the night
4 Tennis great Nadal, to fans
5 One who's always looking for a lift?
6 What a worker who oversleeps will be
7 Christine of "The Blacklist"
8 Eggs in a lab
9 Cry between "ready" and "go!"
10 Diluted, as a drink
11 ___ Goldfinger (Bond villain)
12 Something skipped across a pond
13 Racing vehicles for Anakin Skywalker
18 Nebraska native tribe
21 Martini & ___ (brand of sparkling wine)
22 Rocks from side to side
23 "To be, ___ to be"
24 Photo of Marilyn Monroe, once
26 Last emperor of the Julio-Claudian dynasty
27 Not foul, as a baseball hit
29 Toxic part of cigarettes
32 Uncertainties
33 Licoricelike flavoring
34 Title character who never arrives in a Beckett play
35 Jesse of the Berlin Olympics
37 "___ good in the neighborhood" (restaurant slogan)
38 Volunteer's words
39 Spongy toy material
40 First word of every "Friends" episode title
44 Declared
45 The first "S" in U.S.S.R.
46 Onetime alias of Sean Combs
47 ___ of Wight
48 Thin Russian pancakes

by Ali Gascoigne

49 Places in order of preference
50 Desert stop for camels
52 ___ and proper
54 Prepares to shoot
56 Cousin in the Addams family
57 Arms-loving grp.
58 Little bite
59 Bug mostly seen in winter
60 Peculiar

30

ACROSS

1 Leg muscle, in sports slang
6 Beach lotion letters
9 Grease, informally
13 Tough H.S. science course
14 "If I Could Turn Back Time" singer, 1989
15 Per item
16 "I'm game—just give me the signal"
19 Iowa senator Ernst
20 Kind of cord for a daredevil
21 Emmy-nominated Lucy
23 ___-ray Disc
25 Costa ___
26 Celtics player-turned-executive
29 Snake warning
32 On the open ocean
33 Stitch line
35 Something a pedant picks
36 Cambridge sch.
37 Come before
40 Dallas sch.
41 Prefix with brow
42 Fly majestically
43 Suppress
45 Pots' partners
47 Something to take after a garlicky meal
50 Cinnamony tea
52 1914–18 conflict, for short
53 Broke a fast
54 Get hold of
56 1960s British P.M. ___ Douglas-Home
58 "Let's do it!" . . . or comment on the last words of 16-, 26- and 47-Across, when said together out loud
64 Laundry basketful
65 Horrible person
66 Oreo filler
67 The first "O" in YOLO
68 Scot's "not"
69 Lift up

DOWN

1 Sarcastic laugh syllable
2 Human's closest relative
3 Many a C.F.O.'s degree
4 When the abolition of slavery is commemorated
5 Toy on a string
6 "Thar ___ blows!"
7 Calligraphy tool
8 Naan-like Native American food
9 Cape Canaveral event
10 In quite a spot
11 Yawner
12 Sword's name with two accents
14 "Four-alarm" food
17 Org. for the Indiana Fever and the Atlanta Dream
18 "Yes, Pierre"
21 Sonia Sotomayor, e.g.
22 Like a gut feeling
24 Remove, as a light bulb
26 Block, as a stream
27 Pups' protests
28 "___ whiz!"
30 Biles of the 2016 Olympics
31 Publicity-grabbing move, maybe
34 Go together well
38 Smokey of R&B
39 Body part that might be "sympathetic"
44 Pricey Apple computer
46 Beer-and-lemonade drink
48 Slumbering no more
49 Piece of a mosaic
51 Assistance
54 Flight hub for Norwegian
55 Godsend
57 Per item

by Erik Agard

59 Airport code hidden in FUEL GAUGE
60 Ticked-off feeling
61 Island garland
62 Mornings, for short
63 Court divider

31

ACROSS

1 Closes
6 Like the voice of someone who's stuffed up
11 [Guests must provide their drinks]
15 Went after
16 Sheep-related
17 Where the first presidential caucuses are held
18 "Crossing my fingers!"
19 Squiggly mark in "piñata"
20 Earl __ tea
21 2001 Tom Cruise thriller
23 Some rides from the airport, nowadays
24 Leave out
25 James who sang "At Last"
27 Nickname for former N.B.A. star Darryl Dawkins
35 "Star Wars" princess

36 Maya who designed the Vietnam Veterans Memorial
37 Diamond pattern
38 Suffix with different or confident
39 "Chill out!"
42 Connected PC system
43 Ready to assemble, as a home
45 Reef predator
46 Flowy hair
47 Amy Adams or Emma Stone, hairwise
51 Keep it __ (be honest)
52 Sound from a ghost
53 "What a shame"
56 Kind of ice cream suggested by the starts of 21-, 27- and 47-Across
62 Swear
63 Largest city in South Florida
64 Japanese dog breed

65 "Look how great I did!"
66 Shenanigan
67 Enticed
68 Kill, as a dragon
69 Sits for a photo
70 Venue often named for its sponsor

DOWN

1 Makeshift knife
2 Funny (or sarcastic) joke response
3 Japanese noodle type
4 Pudding ingredient
5 Patron for sailors
6 Friendly response to "Do you mind?"
7 Hertz rival
8 __ Road, route for Marco Polo
9 "Still . . ."
10 Director Spike
11 Beginning of the universe
12 Days of __
13 One with a debt
14 Large inlets
22 Rapper __ Wayne

23 Maneuver upon missing a GPS instruction
26 Take out of the freezer
27 Video excerpts
28 Symbol on a valentine
29 Floating fuel carrier
30 Race official
31 Rear-__ (auto accident)
32 "The Times They Are a-Changin'" singer
33 African antelope
34 Opera singer Fleming
39 Made the sound of a crow
40 Group that inspired "Mamma Mia!"
41 The first modern one was held in Athens in 1896
44 Off in the distance
46 Nickname
48 Pacific weather phenomenon
49 Unfortunate crowd reaction to a performer

by Howard Barkin

50 [I don't know the words to this part]
53 College entrance exams
54 Egg-shaped
55 Mr. Pibb or Dr Pepper
57 Has a nosh
58 French female friend
59 Ocean motion
60 Heaps
61 Nickname for grandma
63 It may include the words "You are here"

ACROSS

1 Fab Four hairdos
5 Spiced tea variety
9 Hail Mary, for one
13 Totally awesome
14 Defense in a snowball fight
15 Chops finely
17 Psychedelic stuff from the Evergreen State?
19 Shrek and Fiona
20 Nash's "two-l" beast
21 Lure
23 A, to Beethoven
24 Inning : baseball :: ___ : curling
26 Underwear from the First State?
28 Gambler's action in the Cornhusker State?
32 Member of Islam's largest branch

33 Tennis serving whiz
34 National Hot Dog Month
37 Music genre for the Village People
39 Calder Cup rink org.
40 Forest animal in the state nicknamed Old Dominion?
42 Ate
43 Opposite of día
45 ___ stick
46 Snow blower maker
47 Birds on Canadian dollar coins
49 Mosquito from the state nicknamed Land of Opportunity?
51 Highway divider in the Centennial State?
54 Mr. Turkey
55 Diamonds, slangily
56 Someone ___ (not mine or yours)

58 Moving around fast
62 Entire range
64 Pasta from the Golden State?
66 Word next to an arrow on a maze
67 Hard ___ (toiling away)
68 Lo-cal
69 Frequent Sicilian erupter
70 Daddy-o
71 © follower, typically

DOWN

1 Whimper
2 October birthstone
3 Tuscany tower site
4 Amount of cream cheese
5 Corporate $$$ overseer
6 Hilarious type
7 Ready for battle
8 Reply to "Who's there?"
9 Jut out
10 Bailed-out insurance giant

11 Attachment you might send to a tech person when you have a computer problem
12 "Whatever!"
16 Some Form 1040 data, for short
18 "You ___ ?" (butler's response)
22 "Mister Rogers' Neighbor-hood" airer
25 ___ vu
27 Magician's name suffix
28 Palindromic bread
29 Navigate like a whale
30 Sign of hospitality
31 Backside
35 British throne?
36 Popular fitness class
38 Dumpster output
40 Blood feud
41 Put in proper piles
44 Something a tired gardener might lean on

by Tom Pepper

46 How wallflowers act
48 The "S" of R.S.V.P.
50 Doofus
51 Pack of butts
52 Music copyright org.
53 Old-fashioned "Cool!"
57 Salon sound
59 Ballet bend
60 "I'd rather go naked than wear fur" grp.
61 Belgian river to the North Sea
63 Coffee dispenser
65 Tiebreaker periods, for short

33

ACROSS

1 Fortuneteller's deck
6 Flabbergasted
10 Material for a rock climber's harness
14 Collective bargaining side
15 ___ Hari (W.W. I spy)
16 Follow orders
17 "Sleep well!"
19 Actress Hathaway of "The Devil Wears Prada"
20 Australia's unofficial national bird
21 Work from Keats or Shelley
22 Nut used to make marzipan
24 Content that has already been shared, as on a Reddit forum
27 Coastal county of England
28 Billy Idol hit that starts "Hey little sister, what have you done?"
32 Bullfighters' entrance march
35 Stroke gently
36 Crankcase fluid
37 Sidestep
38 ___ Enterprise

39 Secret ___ (metaphoric key to success)
41 Pal of Harry and Hermione
42 Corporate money V.I.P.
43 Henrik ___, "Hedda Gabler" playwright
44 Vegetarian spaghetti topper
49 Chicken holders
50 Bears witness (to)
54 Austin Powers, vis-à-vis James Bond
56 ___-Caps (candy)
57 Stocking stuffer?
58 Elderly
59 Graduation garb . . . or what the compound answers to 17-, 28- and 44-Across represent?
63 Birch or beech
64 Astronaut Shepard
65 Elements of a roll call
66 Minute or hour marker on a clock
67 Fey of comedy
68 iPhone maker

DOWN

1 One doing piano repair
2 Japanese cartoon art genre
3 Assemble, as equipment
4 Cry of delight
5 Big bang maker
6 Surrounded by
7 $15/hour, maybe
8 Biblical verb suffix
9 Collection of figures for a statistical analysis
10 Meandered
11 Very annoying
12 Quaker William
13 Took a gander at
18 "Me? Never!"
23 '60s hallucinogenic
25 "Never in the field of human conflict was so much ___ by so many to so few": Churchill
26 Slipper or sandal
27 Females in wool

29 British racing town that lent its name to a kind of salt
30 Pleasant
31 Country/pop singer Campbell
32 Request at a hair salon, informally
33 Last name of a trio of baseball brothers
34 Protection at the beach
38 Crafts in a "close encounter of the third kind"
39 Riverbank deposit
40 Partner of ready and willing
42 "Monkey see, monkey do" type
45 Like some sweatshirts and cobras
46 Item of fishing gear
47 Fruit that's peeled
48 Zillions
51 Crush with the foot, with "on"
52 Low-tech hair dryer
53 Touch, taste or sight

by Leslie Rogers and Andrea Carla Michaels

54 Hiker's route
55 Home of the Taj Mahal
56 Length of a bridge

60 Rumble in the Jungle champ
61 Crime lab material
62 Space between two teeth, e.g.

34

ACROSS

1 Gloomy atmosphere
5 Mess up
9 Subject of some youth sports fraud
12 What inventions start as
14 Actor Morales of "The Brink"
15 Toot one's own horn
16 *Fish fork
17 *Cocktail fork
19 Vice president who became ambassador to Japan
21 Swapped
22 It ends rather spookily: Abbr.
23 Last ruler of the United Kingdoms of Sweden and Norway
26 Often-prewritten news article, for short
29 Regret
30 Wide-eyed sort
34 Unrealized
36 Draw (out)

37 Leslie in the Women's Basketball Hall of Fame
38 *Salad fork
39 Flashlight inserts, perhaps
40 Soldier's topper
41 Well, in old Rome
42 Loos
43 Some rock coverings
44 "Bye!"
45 Wide shoe spec
46 ___ Village (Manhattan neighborhood)
47 Russia, once
50 Preschool group?
53 Estate sharer
56 Bespectacled canine of comics
59 *Dessert fork
62 *Fruit fork
63 Haberdasher's array
64 "Yikes!"
65 TV's Don Draper, for one

66 Abbr. on a remote
67 Fictional boy who rafted down the Mississippi
68 Big brand of petrol

DOWN

1 ___ Beach, Calif.
2 Makeshift
3 Makeshift shelter
4 Kosher bakery no-no
5 They might go viral
6 "Mr. Robot" network
7 Partner of wide
8 What Buddha is said to have meditated under
9 Barren
10 Boarding pass datum
11 "Heavens to Murgatroyd!"
13 Genre of the band Less Than Jake
15 Idiotic
18 The Cards, on scoreboards

20 1980s–'90s N.F.L. great Ronnie
24 Like envelope flaps
25 Relatives of puffins
27 Relatives of kingfishers
28 India ___
31 Wind tunnel currents
32 "Got it!"
33 They can be saturated
34 Pride parade letters
35 Rest ___
39 Big name in laptops
40 Fashion accessory that may be six feet long
42 No longer interested in
43 An assistant might take one
48 Follower of yes or no in the military
49 Ancient arts venue
51 Black-and-white mammals
52 Prefix with musicology

by Jacob Stulberg

53 Security guard's viewing, for short
54 River originating in Pittsburgh
55 Shoe part
57 Figure on a résumé, in brief
58 Monk known as "The Father of English History"
60 Upsilon follower
61 Stop on a trip

35 ★ ★

ACROSS
1 Got the attention of
8 Followers of the Baal Shem Tov
15 Author known for the intelligence of his writing?
16 Outer layer of a membrane
17 Crystallizing substance in Kurt Vonnegut's "Cat's Cradle"
18 Conglomeration
19 & 20 Pattern in back of a window
21 Cut down, possibly
22 Cold-weather product prefix
23 Reading ability?
26 Can't stomach
30 "De profundis," e.g.

32 Best-selling erotic novelist __ Leigh
33 Germ-free state
35 & 37 Hit Leonardo DiCaprio film, with "The"
38 Narrow tube in chemistry
39 Get better
40 App customers
41 Cinches
45 Boardom?
46 Playing card making
49 Word with full or file
50 & 52 Commander at the First Battle of Bull Run
55 Kobe or Shaq, notably
57 Recruits
58 Steam locomotive workers

59 Black Panther's co-creator
60 Reduction of tension
61 Choir composition

DOWN
1 Chasséd, say
2 Withdraw
3 Gets a 5 on an A.P. exam, say
4 One who may help you keep your balance?
5 Lancastrian or Liverpudlian
6 __ Laszlo (cosmetics brand)
7 Not easily understood
8 Stacks
9 Lumberjack
10 Daytime TV fare
11 Pass the time
12 Prepare, as hides for tanning

13 Org. that supported the Good Friday Agreement
14 "Scrumptious!"
24 Razor cut
25 May and others, for short
27 Hard to hear, perhaps
28 Quick pace
29 A good one is hard to crack
31 Underground activity
33 1970 Australian Open winner
34 W.W. II weapon
35 Full of sass
36 Gap in a schedule
38 Lightweight boxer?
42 Brawl in the backwoods
43 Possible candidate for a Razzie Award

by Timothy Polin

44 Has a funny feeling
47 Like atoms with complete valance shells
48 Inherently
51 Stomach
52 The new girl on Fox's "New Girl"
53 Disfavoring
54 Group with a tartan
55 Subject of many '60s hits?
56 Had something

ACROSS

1 Gold, frankincense and myrrh, famously
6 Fleet of foot
11 Bit of bunny slope gear
13 Pop music's __ Vanilli
14 #1 hit for the Troggs
16 Finalize, as comic art
17 Pandora released them
18 Pupil's place
19 Speaks like Sylvester
20 Face cards, informally?
21 N.Y.C. subway line
22 Bed size
24 Bad outcome for a QB: Abbr.
25 Reacting to an awkward moment, perhaps
29 Jazz improvisations
32 Flashy accessories
33 Aperitif with black currant liqueur
34 Mother of Horus
35 Threshold
36 Pasta choice
37 With 38-Across, cocktail with lemon or lime
38 See 37-Across
39 Center
40 Oppressive
42 Removable locks
43 What Gollum calls "my precious"
44 Number of suspects in Clue
45 J. Edgar Hoover's org.
48 Parsley portion
51 J. Edgar Hoover used one: Abbr.
53 Old letter opener
54 Source of the word "whiskey"
55 Close, as a community
57 Touch of color
58 Sounding like Big Ben
59 Many Punjabis
60 Quick cuts

DOWN

1 Breathers?
2 Unaffiliated voters: Abbr.
3 See 14-Down
4 Item shot out of a cannon at an arena
5 Evade
6 Like the Cheshire cat
7 Entertaining, in a way
8 Sorts
9 Go gaga (over)
10 Spam holders
11 Not so hot
12 Reggae singer __ Kamoze
14 With 3-Down, Nintendo exercise offering
15 Part of a guitar that also names something you can wear
21 Stand-__
23 Instant
24 Possibilities
25 Static __
26 "It's a joke"
27 Petty criticisms
28 Moxie
29 Oil machinery
30 "Oh, really?"
31 Over, to Odette
32 "Show me your worst!"
35 Russian pancake
36 Start of some evasive maneuvering
38 Deliberate discourtesies
39 Verb that's also a Roman numeral
41 Otto who worked on the Manhattan Project
42 Word before reach or reason
44 Venice's Bridge of __
45 Original sauna users
46 Water cooler?
47 Loyal follower?
48 Gathers dust

by Trenton Charlson

49 Toyota hybrids, jocularly
50 Zamboni site
52 Actor Cage, to friends
53 Pass on
56 "Didn't need to know that!"

37

ACROSS

1 Italian scooter
6 Endurance
10 Glimpses
15 Like a necktie near the end of a long workday, maybe
16 Big name in cosmetics
17 Another nickname for the Governator
18 Bass group?
19 Give stars to
20 Prize that comes with 9 million kronor
21 Kidnapper who gets arrested?
24 Page listing
25 Once-over
26 Soccer player Hamm
27 Measure of purity
29 Win a one-on-one game against a Toronto hoops player?
34 Army allowance
37 Gun-shy
38 Spiffy top
39 Even up
40 Partner of pieces
41 Elates
42 Long time out?
43 Not altogether
44 Playwright Sean who wrote "The Plough and the Stars"
45 "I don't want this house after all"?
48 Japanese box meal
49 Group of traffic cops, for short?
50 ___ economy
53 E'en if
55 Synagogue singer with hokey humor?
59 Pizazz
61 "No problem at all!"
62 Eastern European capital
63 Hoffman who wrote "Steal This Book"
64 What photocopiers do
65 Church chorus
66 Gave a pill, say
67 River whose name comes entirely from the last eight letters of the alphabet
68 Sacred text . . . or your reaction upon figuring out this puzzle's theme?

DOWN

1 Oklahoma's ___ Air Force Base
2 Attempt
3 FaceTime alternative
4 Confined, with "up"
5 "You've got to be kidding me!"
6 Mustang catcher
7 "Dear ___ Hansen" (2017 Tony winner)
8 Dark kind of look
9 Some court wear
10 Oh, what an actress!
11 Tennis ___
12 Things in the backs of Macs
13 Theater seating info
14 What bears do in the market
22 "The Last Jedi" director Johnson
23 Not a single
28 Show up
29 Galoot
30 How this clue appears
30 How this clue appears
31 ___ yoga
32 Like some shoppes
33 Optimistic
34 Billiards need
35 It's a relief
36 Ticking dangers
40 Margaret Thatcher, e.g., in her later years
41 Derides
43 James who sang at the opening of the 1984 Summer Olympics
44 "Beetle Bailey" dog

by Jeff Slutzky and Derek Bowman

46 Crept (along)
47 Need to speak
50 Many an intern
51 Skater Slutskaya
52 Grind, in a way
53 Mr. with a "Wild Ride" at Disneyland
54 Drifter
56 Savoir-faire
57 Anthem starter
58 Italy's Lake __
60 Pizza delivery

38

ACROSS

1 Lid attachment
5 Mixes in
9 Make art on glass or metal
13 Billy the Kid vis-à-vis Henry McCarty
15 Lecherous person
16 Boutique-filled N.Y.C. neighborhood
17 "___, do these jeans make me look fat?"
19 Perfectly
20 "You're oversharing!"
21 Levine of Maroon 5
22 Big swigs
23 Part of a movie that can be spoiled
25 "___! The flight attendant just swatted a bug!"
28 Smooth sailing site
30 Place with treatments
31 Club with travel advice, for short
32 Pay attention to
33 Mark that's just above average
35 Place where you can get stuck
36 "___, would you like to purchase some religious music?"
40 Not just any
43 Peer through a window, maybe
44 Myriad
48 Mr. Rogers
49 The Na'vi in "Avatar," e.g.
50 Meet (with) at midday, say
53 "___ and those crazy sheep costumes!"
56 Bakery-cafe chain
57 Bikini part
58 Actor Neeson
60 "On the other hand . . ."
61 Where Paris took Helen
62 "___! Petr, I'm begging you again to let me get this!"
65 Break in the action
66 Really cool, in slang
67 "Me, too!"
68 Slippery
69 Teensy
70 Harness racing gait

DOWN

1 Research assistant, informally
2 Female graduates
3 Not get used
4 Makeshift receptacle for ballots
5 "O mio babbino caro," e.g.
6 Foundational teachings
7 "Obviously, Sherlock!"
8 Wimbledon unit
9 First name in perfumes
10 Windows strip
11 The Louvre, originally
12 Spot where one might get grilled
14 Some origami birds
18 Advantage
22 Quarry noise
24 Website for film buffs
26 Upscale kitchen feature
27 Told, as tales
29 Hacker's goal
34 Fraternity letter
37 Exhaust
38 Dubious Tibetan sighting
39 Ostracize
40 Part of a bridge
41 "Amen!"
42 "Puh-leeze!," in facial form
45 Lease term, often
46 Loud subgenre of punk
47 "Bingo!"
51 Colorful fish
52 Genie holders

by Bruce Haight

54 In a jovial way
55 Choose
59 Ugh-worthy
62 TV drama of 2000–15
63 Benzoyl peroxide target, informally
64 Fate

39

ACROSS

1 Made jokes
7 Slim amphibian
11 Genre for Jay-Z and Master P
14 Relative of a llama
15 "Damn right!"
17 Carnegie __
18 Two tablespoons
19 Shovel's go-with
20 Performances with no ac-companiment
22 Mostly bygone airline amenity
23 Many a Clint Eastwood role
25 Bay of __, body separating Spain and France
27 Chick of jazz
28 Plea at sea
30 Jumping-off points?
31 "The Simpsons" clown

33 Brexit land
35 Govt. ID
36 E.M.T., at times
38 Dict. listing
41 One interred in Red Square
42 Line on a weather map
44 Sated for now, with "over"
47 "Thelma & Louise" studio
49 "Scat!"
50 Disquiet
52 Attends without a date
54 Toboggan, e.g.
55 Yugoslav-American tennis great
57 __ Major
58 Question that might be answered "Muy bien, y usted?"
60 Belgian brew, familiarly
62 Movie franchise that set a record opening weekend gross in 2018 ($640 million)

63 Be visibly precarious
64 Neighbor of Homer
65 Dumb __ (oafs)
66 Feels

DOWN

1 Fills to the gills
2 Some Nellies and Noras, formally
3 Printing of a magazine with two different covers, e.g.
4 Counts
5 Green prefix
6 Matisse's "La __"
7 What Alice goes through to find "Jabber-wocky" printed backward
8 Baylor's home
9 Quite wee
10 Home of the Tisch Sch. of the Arts
11 "The magic word"

12 Epic that opens "Of arms and the man I sing . . ."
13 Geometric diamonds
16 Meme feline
21 Hosp. areas
24 Animosities
26 Hindu retreats
29 Aspen or Tahoe
32 Urge
34 Always, to a bard
37 Pep
38 Prognosticated
39 One taken by the arm
40 Grosses out
41 Entice
43 Volcanic rocks
44 Native of Florence, e.g.
45 Head over heels
46 Judged
48 Ending with Fannie or Ginnie
51 County in England or New Jersey
53 Leaders before 41-Across

by Ross Trudeau

56 French "to be"
59 Maniacal leader?
61 Big name in denim

40 ★ ★

ACROSS

1 Grouch
5 Some lines drawn with protractors
9 Airbnb alternative
14 Miller ___
15 One nabbed by the fuzz
16 With eyes open
17 Trotter's course
18 Marquee performer
19 Shot down
20 Maternity ward worker who counts each day's births?
23 First pope to be called "the Great"
24 Great
25 Noncollegiate fraternity member
28 Dairy item thrown in a food fight?
32 Snake's warning
35 Navy rank below lt. junior grade
36 Fry up
37 Quick rests
40 Dined on humble pie
42 One selling a Super Bowl spot, say
43 MSNBC competitor
44 Tampa-to-Jacksonville dir.
45 Dynamite?
50 Thesaurus offering: Abbr.
51 "___ we go again . . ."
52 Lava below the surface
56 Like 20-, 28- and 45-Across vis-à-vis the female-sounding phrases they're based on?
60 "___ at 'em!"
62 Cat with no tail
63 Latin music great Puente
64 Look forward to
65 ___ bowl (trendy healthful food)
66 Last word said just before opening the eyes
67 Parts of volcanoes
68 Foe of Russia, with "the"
69 Where a bell is rung M-F at 9:30 a.m. and 4:00 p.m.

DOWN

1 Thickheaded sorts
2 Stud on a pair of jeans
3 In the slightest
4 Agnostic's lack
5 Place to pray
6 Prepares for a second career, say
7 Boxful for a kindergartner
8 Activated, as a trap
9 Unit of measurement for a horse's height equivalent to four inches
10 Scraped knee, in totspeak
11 Annual filing
12 Barely win, with "out"
13 Commanded
21 Radio dial: Abbr.
22 Girl entering society, in brief
26 Pretend
27 Group organizing a Mardi Gras parade
29 "Sure is!"
30 Operate
31 Sea-___ (Washington airport)
32 Coverings of cuts
33 "Alas . . ."
34 Dictator
38 Unopened
39 Kwik-E-Mart storekeeper
40 Cell tower equipment
41 Cable airer of N.B.A. games
43 Monaco Grand Prix, e.g.
46 Successful defender, in academia
47 Granny, in the South
48 Land-bound bird
49 Wicker material
53 In need of a good scrubbing

by Amanda Chung and Karl Ni

54 Ones to share a pint with
55 Without company
57 Give off
58 Trawlers' equipment
59 On-ramp's opposite
60 Washroom, informally
61 Homophone of "you" that shares no letters with it

41 ★ ★

ACROSS

1 First U.S. color TVs
5 Shooter's need
8 Believers in oneness
14 "Spamalot" lyricist
16 Post-flood locale
17 One stuck abroad?
18 Frame of reference
19 Professor to Harry Potter
20 Follower of "My country"
22 Raiding grp.
23 It can make an impression in correspondence
26 Risk-free
29 Lacking a mate
32 Fit for a queen
34 Key
37 British record label
41 "I'm out"
44 Unlikely source of a Top 40 song
45 Popular Greek dish
46 Surrounds
49 On the blue side, for short
50 Ottoman
53 ___ beetle
56 Clay, after conversion
57 Call to reserve?
59 Calrissian of "Star Wars"
63 Traffic enforcement device
66 Adoring looks seen 10 times in this puzzle's grid
69 Curfew, maybe
70 Lickety-split
71 Revenue-raising measure
72 "Neato!"
73 Branch of Islam

DOWN

1 Guns
2 Sing sentimentally
3 Work whose title character is buried alive
4 Equipment in an ice cream shop
5 Rabblement
6 In a bad way
7 Annual spring occurrence
8 Instrument that opens Stravinsky's "The Rite of Spring"
9 Homer's path
10 "I bet!"
11 To the stern
12 "Same here!"
13 Several lines of music?
15 "Bonne ___!"
21 "___ ever . . ."
24 Playfully roguish
25 Where photosynthesis occurs
27 ___-slipper (flower)
28 Commoners
29 Eight: Prefix
30 Wilt
31 Superserious
33 Grabs (onto)
35 Ones pumped up for a race?
36 "That's beyond me"
38 Dressed
39 Sam of R&B
40 Not know from ___ (be clueless about)
42 Some deer
43 Closet-y smell
47 Freon, for one
48 Sierra Nevada product
50 Side
51 "C'est magnifique!"
52 Competitor of Citizen
54 Standoffish
55 Iona College athletes
58 Cry after a hectic week
60 When doubled, a taunt
61 South Asian living abroad
62 Org. for some inspectors
64 ___ Air, carrier to Taiwan

by Stu Ockman

65 Supporting
letter, informally
67 A Chaplin
68 Gossip

ACROSS

1 "Aladdin" prince
4 Sandal feature
10 Flat-bottomed boat
14 Scoundrel
15 Beekeeper's locale
16 Sharpen, as one's skills
17 N.Y. engineering sch.
18 *They get stuffed at Greek restaurants
20 Enemies from way back
22 Consider carefully
23 *With 50-Across, classic ice cream treats
24 Judge's seat
25 Louis, par exemple
27 Something divided in W.W. II
28 Stand for a speaker
30 *With 44-Across, sour candies
32 Body image, briefly
33 Ages and ages
34 Tribal emblems
35 Unproductive . . . or, literally, a hint to the answers to this puzzle's starred clues
37 Not yet bankrupt
40 Goal for an actor
41 Maidenform garment
44 *See 30-Across
45 Noted 1970s–'80s Gang leader?
46 Revolutions can divide them
47 Dallas hoopster, for short
48 Wedding gown designer Di Santo
50 *See 23-Across
52 __ Beanies (bygone toys)
54 Super conductor?
55 *Garnishes for old-fashioneds
57 Subway unit
58 Cargo's place
59 Keep tabs on tabbies, say
60 Breast Cancer Awareness mo.
61 Murder : crows :: parliament : __
62 Carves
63 French possessive

DOWN

1 One going head over heels?
2 Seaport near Buenos Aires
3 Emphatic denial
4 Add, as an extra
5 Dispersed
6 Madres' sisters
7 Kendrick Lamar's genre
8 South American corn cakes
9 Air race marker
10 Roe source
11 Soldier's request before entering a firefight
12 Like quaint schoolhouses
13 Anderson who directed "Isle of Dogs"
19 Wall off
21 Relatives, casually
24 Paris eateries
26 Connections
29 Indie artist DiFranco
31 U.F.O. occupants
33 Blackboard chore
34 Emulates Pinocchio
35 One dressed to impress
36 British bathroom
37 Naval bigwig: Abbr.
38 Home to many Greeks, informally
39 Score at the start of a set
41 The original "The Office," e.g.
42 Wearying routine
43 Puts in order
45 Not give up on
46 They loop the Loop

by Emily Carroll

49 One crying "Uncle!," perhaps

51 Raid targets

53 Partner of odds

54 Fit together well

55 "What have we here?!"

56 Abbr. sometimes written twice in a row

43 ⭐ ⭐

ACROSS

1 Intelligible
9 Ticker test, for short
12 Leaves after dinner?
15 Formal defense
16 Homing (in on)
18 68-Down
20 Tropical black bird
21 Number between cinque and sette
22 Economic crisis
23 Exploit
25 Sporty auto feature
27 Commercial lead-in to film
31 Let in or let on
33 Novelty singer/ songwriter ___ Sherman
36 Symbol in the logo of the Democratic Socialists of America
37 Starting
39 Pile for a record company exec
41 Cancel
42 68-Down with a "/" inside it
46 Like 2001
47 Relative whose name sounds like a city in France
48 "Didn't you get the ___?"
49 Capital on the Dnieper
51 Giggly outburst
53 Development sites
56 One loitering
58 Suffix with psych-
60 Term of address in "The Wizard of Id"
61 Right-hand page
64 Palindromic relative
66 Carpet quality
67 68-Down with a "∘" after it
72 Steak accompanier
73 Like many classical statues
74 Some I.R.S. forms
75 Dispirited
76 Send

DOWN

1 Powerhouse in curling
2 Went on first
3 Game show host with a shaved head
4 Cambridgeshire cathedral city
5 Bush critters
6 Old plume source
7 1986 Elton John love song
8 Lab instructors, often
9 Book after II Chronicles
10 Sharp
11 Holy ___
12 Quinceañera attendee, perhaps
13 Expire
14 At least 35, for a U.S. president
17 Transpire
19 Alternative to TGI Fridays
24 CD part
26 Traditional
28 Timeshare unit, often
29 Section of The Economist
30 Fetching

32 Bugs Bunny or Jessica Rabbit
34 Self-reflective question
35 Standard
38 Move like a moth
40 Mishmash
42 Aesir trickster
43 Terse admission
44 Once named
45 Med. insurance groups
50 Vice ___
52 Former Disney exec Michael
54 Soccer star Chastain
55 Snow White's housemates, for instance
57 🐴 + A + 🐗 for catalogs, e.g.
59 Summation symbol, in math
62 Part of a white script on a red can
63 Not up or down
65 Short drive
67 Hem's partner
68 Palindromic number

by Peter A. Collins

69 Predecessor of
the C.I.A.
70 German 101
verb
71 Carry-___
(some luggage)

ACROSS

1 It emerges at dawn
4 Prometheus' gift
8 May honoree
14 "Either you do it ___ will"
15 Russia's ___ Mountains
16 Source of some pop-ups
17 Contribution of Gilbert, but not Sullivan
19 Give a hand to
20 Implore
21 "___ from that . . ."
23 Presided over
24 Word of greeting
26 Help for a star witness?
28 Underground rock
29 Dawn's direction
30 Sound from a rowdy crowd
31 Like Ganymede among Jupiter's moons
34 Light beige
37 Classify by type
38 "Otello" and "Pagliacci"

42 Many a character in Ann M. Martin's "The Baby-Sitters Club"
44 Language of the answers to this puzzle's uniclues
45 Urban area
48 British bottom
50 Cpl. or sgt.
51 Comment made while yawning
54 Prime-time time
56 Miley Cyrus's "Party in the ___"
57 One of Donald Trump Jr.'s parents
58 World Smile Day mo.
59 Hair-coloring technique
61 Fight finisher
65 Any of the Magi
66 Nessie's home
67 Where you might get into hot water
68 Dissuades

69 "When all ___ fails . . ."
70 How many feet are in a fathom

DOWN

1 [See note]
2 Sch. with a campus in Providence
3 Dainty eaters
4 [See note]
5 N.Y.C. subway letters
6 Rapping sound
7 Runs off to a justice of the peace
8 [See note]
9 "Awake and Sing!" playwright Clifford
10 Bygone Pan Am rival
11 Call to the hounds
12 Port up the lake from Cleveland, O.
13 Clarify, as butter
18 Seminary subj.
22 Old person, in Oldenburg
24 [See note]

25 Notable stretches
27 Sadistic
29 [See note]
32 "Somebody That I Used to Know" singer, 2011
33 Byron's "before"
35 Alternative to a cup
36 Dungeons & Dragons, for one, in brief
39 Carnival game with bottles
40 Author Sholem
41 Drinking game penalty, perhaps
43 "Peter Pan" dog
44 [See note]
45 [See note]
46 Good place to be during a blizzard
47 It might be left holding the bag
49 Annoy
52 One practicing self-help, informally

by Queena Mewers and Alex Eaton-Salners

53 Declares with confidence
54 [See note]
55 ___ factor
60 Dr. of rap
62 Facility at Quantico, Va.: Abbr.
63 News inits. since 1958
64 Line on a receipt

45 ★ ★

ACROSS

1 Wrangler, for one
5 Things kids sometimes draw
9 Carriages in Kew Gardens
14 Band with a slash in its name
15 Occur to, with "on"
16 ___ Cinemas, second-largest theater chain in the U.S.
17 Be hot under the collar
18 Snap, Crackle and Pop, e.g.
19 Dweller on the Arabian Sea
20 "No one can get in a fight by himself," informally
23 Rum cocktail
25 Robert Burns's "since"
26 Starting point for a platypus
27 Steam
28 Some Windows systems
30 Is nostalgic for

32 Classic song with the lyric "I'll see you in my dreams"
36 What you may call it?
37 S. Amer. land
38 Air condition?
42 World traveler since 1985
47 What's honed on the range?
50 Put pressure on
51 Downed a sub?
52 Goethe's "The ___-King"
53 Like the German article "der": Abbr.
56 Welled (up)
58 Flip out . . . or a hint to eight answers in this puzzle
61 Diamond datum
62 Adjutant
63 Progenitor of the Edomites, in the Bible
66 Old Scottish title
67 What optical readers do

68 Staples of "Poor Richard's Almanack"
69 Sir William ___, medical pioneer
70 Far from subtle actors
71 Pro side

DOWN

1 Dig, in a way
2 Writer Umberto ___
3 Where Copy and Paste appear
4 School tech class site
5 Some expensive dental work
6 Rows
7 Jerks
8 Having a white blanket
9 Body building block
10 San ___, Italy
11 Banded stones
12 Get along
13 Babies in a pond
21 Powerful checker
22 "I'll spring for it"

23 National park in Utah
24 Latin word on a dollar bill
29 Pipe part
31 Basted, e.g.
33 Indigenous Peruvian
34 Whack
35 Littlest piggy
39 "My assumption is . . ."
40 Time of day, in ads
41 Archived document
43 Current device
44 Delivery door location, often
45 Silky cottons
46 Fired
47 Opposite of staccato
48 Foams
49 Universal
54 Supply that no one's supposed to find
55 Second-longest-running Broadway musical ever (after "The Phantom of the Opera")

by Morton J. Mendelson

57 A very long time back
59 Provider of directions to a farmer
60 Mild cheese
64 Wow
65 ___ Constitution

ACROSS

1 Bridge
5 "I'll take care of that"
9 American Girl products
14 Jai ___
15 Common blessing
17 Undercover buster
18 Rhyming description for IHOP's "Fresh 'N Fruity" pancakes
19 Safety warning for some kitchenware
21 Born
22 ___ Park, Calif.
23 Jots
26 Outer thigh stabilizers, in brief
29 See in court, say
30 Art Spiegelman's Pulitzer-winning graphic novel
31 Craze
34 Road Runner cartoon sights
38 Goof

39 Warm and cozy spots
41 Manning with two Super Bowl M.V.P. awards
42 Homeland of many 2010s refugees
44 What bugs are found in
45 Bug on a hook, maybe
46 Ctrl-___-Del
48 On the loose
50 Big news involving extraterrestrials
54 Caddies' suggestions
55 Some four-year degrees, for short
56 Kangaroo's pouch
59 Loudly angry, as a group
62 Flight part
64 Rolls the dice and moves one's token
65 Perfect dives

66 Parts of porch chairs
67 Airport postings, in brief
68 Italian wine region

DOWN

1 Lead-in to Francisco or Pedro
2 With 36-Down, astronomical rarity . . . or a hint to the circled letters
3 Alexander Hamilton's nemesis
4 ___ Maduro, successor to Venezuela's Hugo Chávez
5 Fairy tale baddie
6 Sign gas
7 Gets tagged, say
8 Rwandan minority
9 Banned insecticide
10 "Well, well, well!"
11 Sierra ___
12 Some Millers

13 Bad eye sight?
16 Nabokov's nos
20 Part of many German names
22 They act in silence
24 Big name in antacids
25 Meade's opponent at Gettysburg
27 "Dr." of hip-hop
28 Onetime Volvo alternative
32 Master's seeker's hurdle, for short
33 Suffix with oper-
35 Shipping lanes
36 See 2-Down
37 Browser history contents
39 "Freeze!"
40 Fedora, for one
43 McKellen who played Gandalf
45 One who won't serve the average joe
47 Florida city on a bay
49 Back talk
50 Ear passage

by Ross Trudeau

51 Japanese city on a bay
52 ___ blanche
53 Prey for a brown bear
55 Smithereens
57 Actress Ramirez of "Grey's Anatomy"
58 Cremation containers
60 Pull in
61 ___ Intrepid (New York City tourist attraction)
63 Letter after "X"

47

ACROSS

1 Flip (out)
4 Dandy neckwear
10 "___ NewsHour"
13 Opera that famously ends with the line "La commedia è finita!"
15 Potion container
16 NOTED TENOR
17 "Dark Angel" star Jessica
18 Advantage
19 Kickstarter figure
20 Desk tray labels
21 SIMPLE DIET
24 "Dallas Buyers Club" Oscar winner
26 Apprehend
29 Something checked on a questionnaire
30 One of the five founding nations of the Iroquois Confederacy
35 Fat remover, for short
36 Some bathroom postings . . . or what the clues to 16-, 21-, 46- and 59-Across are?
39 Not stuffy
40 Mason's tool
41 "Watch it!"
42 Puzzle
44 Part of the Spanish conjugation of "to be"
46 GET SPEARED
51 Dune transport
53 Verve
54 First car to offer seatbelts (1950)
58 Ilhan ___, one of the first two Muslim women elected to Congress
59 DOOR DECALS
61 Goes from liquid to solid, say
62 Babbling
63 Show with noted alumni, for short
64 "See ya!"
65 Off-roader, in brief

DOWN

1 Out of the strike zone, in a way
2 Product whose introduction was music to people's ears?
3 Group of friends
4 Abbr. in a cockpit
5 The Alamo had a famous one
6 "Can you ___?" (classic cologne catchphrase)
7 The planets, e.g.
8 Immune system defender
9 ___ Toby, character in "Twelfth Night"
10 Part of a stove
11 Pakistani restaurant owner on "Seinfeld"
12 Blind spot?
14 "Whither ___ thou?": John 16:5
15 Milli ___ (1980s–'90s pop duo)
20 "Methinks," in texts
22 [It's gone!]
23 Words of empathy
24 When repeated, a classic of garage rock
25 Teeny-tiny
27 Nighttime woe
28 Like the dawn sky
29 Lead-in to load or lift
31 Our: Fr.
32 Overthrow, e.g.
33 Court oath affirmation
34 Morning coat
37 ___ Rockefeller
38 Where to see two runners side by side
43 Serpentine swimmer
45 What to call un hombre
47 State flower of Indiana
48 Candied
49 Heaviest of the noble gases
50 Pepper used in mole sauce

by John E. Bennett and Jeff Chen

51 Teeth not connected to jaws
52 "And how!"
55 On the briny
56 Elated
57 LG product
59 "Spare" part
60 ___ Wallace, "Ben-Hur" author

48

ACROSS

1 "Not so!"
8 Modifier for "film" or "pinot"
12 *Instructions for premade dinner rolls
14 *Noble couple
15 With 4-Down, each year
16 Election day in the U.S.: Abbr.
17 Workplaces for scrub nurses, for short
18 Wrestling combos
21 Come through in the ___
24 Completely mistaken
25 With 38-Across, hex that's hard to shake
26 Cotton gin inventor Whitney
27 Have the wheel
28 Holier-___-thou
30 Partiality
31 *Latin American side dish that combines two food staples
34 *Title pair in a 2004–07 Nickelodeon sitcom

37 Practically an eternity
38 See 25-Across
39 Set aside for later
43 Bath tissue layer
44 Earth Day's mo.
45 Word of caution
46 Items scattered on bridal paths
48 Almond-flavored liqueur
50 Cool, in dated slang
51 Ancient kingdom in modern-day Jordan
52 Sn, to chemists
53 *Eponymous founders of a Massachusetts-based firearms manufacturer
58 *Duo of magicians who are the longest-running headliners in Las Vegas history
59 Bit of pond scum
60 Mark ___, longtime game show partner of Bill Todman

DOWN

1 Rankle
2 Sock tip
3 Try to hit, as a fly
4 See 15-Across
5 Fills a cargo hold
6 Unaffiliated voters: Abbr.
7 URL ending associated with the beginnings of the answers to the six starred clues
8 P.M. who inspired a 1960s jacket
9 Trilogy of tragedies by Aeschylus
10 I.C.U. drippers
11 Hi-___ monitor
12 Enter to steal from
13 Upbraid
14 Gave out hands
15 School support grps.
19 Shakes one's booty
20 Unnervingly strange
21 Positive kind of attitude
22 Extended family

23 Sound of contemptuous disapproval
25 Hootenanny instrument
28 Barbershop quartet voice
29 Pilgrimage to Mecca
30 "Act like you're supposed to!"
32 Sleeps in a tent, say
33 Rigel or Spica, by spectral type
34 Johnny of 2005's "Charlie and the Chocolate Factory"
35 Part to play
36 "Can I get you ___?"
40 Casino patron
41 Language of 15-Across 4-Down
42 School founded by Henry VI
44 ___ male
45 Caravan animals
47 Insurance giant based in Hartford
48 Supplement
49 Cut the lawn
51 Prefix meaning "within"

by Byron Walden

53 Employer of a
   masseur
54 Brooks with
   Emmy,
   Grammy,

Oscar and
Tony awards
55 "Brokeback
   Mountain"
   director Lee

56 ___-pitch
   softball
57 One of 100 in
   D.C.: Abbr.

49

ACROSS

1 Precursor to riches, it's said
5 "A Farewell to Arms" subj.
8 Snide chuckle
12 Unalaskan, e.g.
14 Hide-y holes?
15 Player of X in "X-Men"
17 Alternatives to texts
18 Squeeze (out)
19 Frequent favorite
21 Scotch brand
23 Courtroom V.I.P.s
24 Part of some future planning, for short
25 Like many of Pindar's works
26 Player of M in "GoldenEye"
29 Carefully listening (to)
32 Screw up
33 Player of V in "V for Vendetta"
36 Cabinet dept. concerned with farming
37 Chicago landmark nicknamed for its resemblance to a legume
39 Player of J in "Men in Black"
43 Urban portmanteau
45 Lead-in to -cide
46 Equal
47 Would really rather not
49 Member of a fratlike Silicon Valley work environment
52 "Game of Thrones" role __ Snow
53 Cardi B's genre
54 15-, 26-, 33- or 39-Across, punnily?
57 Answer to the old riddle "What wears more clothing in summer than in winter?"
58 What Dante wrote in
59 Try to get a good look
60 Crosses out
61 A really long time

DOWN

1 Spanish fleet?
2 San Francisco Bay city
3 Becomes involved in
4 Big __
5 Ones going down in flames?
6 Shake, maybe
7 Walk-__
8 Julia Ward __, writer of "The Battle Hymn of the Republic"
9 Really long times
10 Contained by this text
11 Ph-neutral vitamin brand
13 Mezzanine, e.g.
14 Magical basin used to view one's memories in the Harry Potter books
16 Disgusting sort
20 "Lah-di-__!"
22 Honest-to-goodness
23 Cool woman, jocularly
26 Typical Seder attendee
27 Tiny amount
28 Rutherford known as "The Father of Nuclear Physics"
30 Popular boots from Australia
31 Title role for Sally Field
34 "How relaxing!"
35 Online handle for an Xbox player
38 Zero
39 Drippy, say
40 Geographical feature of Mars
41 12-time Olympic swimming medalist Ryan
42 Classic Camaro, informally
44 Action-documenting cameras
47 Some circle dances
48 Super-uptight

by Sam Trabucco

50 Title creature in an Aesop fable

51 Title in Uncle Remus stories

52 "Black Swan" jump

55 Two for the show, informally?

56 Org. concerned with bugs and plants

50 ★ ★

ACROSS

1 Do some digging
6 "Good joke!"
10 Phishing scheme, e.g.
14 City whose cathedral is the subject of a series of Monet paintings
15 "Good gravy!"
16 Target of the U.S.-backed Radio Martí
17 Exuded
18 Was afraid of losing
20 Pre-22-Across
22 Go for a stroll
23 Indian bread
24 One who gets booked, informally
26 Pre-29-Across
29 Subject in acting school
32 Features of leopards
33 Noted family of German composers
34 Ceiling
36 Some Craigslist listings: Abbr.

37 Red Scare epithet
38 Animal also called a Nittany lion
39 '70s rock?
40 Some Spanish murals
41 Bud of baseball
42 Pre-44-Across
44 Job in a monastery
45 Inauguration recitation
46 Enjoy a nice long bath
47 Pre-50-Across
50 How emotionally developed people handle things
54 One cabinet in a kitchen, typically
56 Douglas ___, author of "The Hitchhiker's Guide to the Galaxy"
58 ___ boots
59 Pod creature
60 Regal maker

61 Flabbergast
62 "All right already!"
63 Skunk's defense

DOWN

1 Positive
2 Thatcher's creation
3 Anise-flavored liqueur
4 Bar snack
5 Causes (oneself) to be cherished
6 Long-beaked bird
7 Soup thickener
8 Doesn't just choose randomly
9 Autoplaying annoyances, sometimes
10 Dish that can give you garlic breath
11 Park place?
12 Ferrara who directed "King of New York"
13 Wasn't late for
19 Supermarket aids
21 Extremely, informally

25 Auto-reply?
26 "Stat!"
27 Increased
28 The Teflon Don
29 Virgil's fellow traveler
30 Eyelike openings
31 Desert in southern Africa
33 Prominent Gorbachev feature
35 Part of a website
37 Scotch flavorer
38 Suddenly got excited
40 Hotel sojourns
41 Pharaonic symbols
43 ___ Whitehead, author of the 2017 Pulitzer-winning novel "The Underground Railroad"
44 Tiny amount
46 Brunch partner of 47-Down
47 Brunch partner of 46-Down
48 Very often

by Will Nediger

49 Italian word with a grave accent that becomes a brand name with an acute accent

51 With the bow, in music

52 Where a supervillain schemes

53 Gay anthem of 1978

55 Romantically pursue

57 Where a telescope points

51

ACROSS

1 Crowd on the move
6 Valuable paper
14 Crossing the keel
15 It holds water
16 Blue jays
18 "Watch out!"
19 Game with 501 points
20 ___ plate
21 Temple title
24 Bygone compacts
26 Honey bees
30 "I can see clearly now"
31 Second-largest moon of Saturn
32 Alternative to AOL
33 Dry eyes
38 Abbr. at a tire shop
41 To boot
42 Autobahn auto
46 High seas
51 Candy bar with chocolate and caramel around a wafer
52 Tributary of the Rio Grande
53 Gandhi and others, for short
54 Much of the back of a baseball card
57 Follower of debate in the General Assembly, in brief
59 Green peas
63 AA and AAA
64 Farm refrain
65 Parts of tourist guides
66 Jobs at a body shop

DOWN

1 Leon Uris novel, with "The"
2 Shortest Old Testament book
3 Smooths over
4 Very, informally
5 Albert Einstein, notably
6 'L' train overseer, for short
7 Caterer's container
8 Funny Foxx
9 Indian chief
10 Surface
11 Thunder, but not Lightning
12 Bleeps
13 QB's accumulation: Abbr.
15 Nikola Tesla's countrymen
17 ___ miss
20 Not yet on the sched.
22 Without exception
23 Like a crisp picture, say
25 Private info, for short
27 "There but for the grace of God ___"
28 Opus ___
29 Kick out for good
34 Real heel
35 Seat of White Pine County, Nev.
36 "Now!"
37 China's Chiang ___ -shek
38 Election fig.
39 Unlikely source of a silk purse
40 Mirror
43 Lots of
44 Teacher's punishment
45 Magazine no.
47 Tough-to-win horse racing bet
48 Certain intimate apparel sizes
49 Traffic director
50 Got back (to)
55 Abound
56 Tegan and ___ (pop duo)
58 Andy Taylor's kid on old TV
59 Keglers' org.
60 Quick drink

by Randolph Ross

61 Paris's Jardin
___ Tuileries
62 Kind of pad

52 ★ ★

ACROSS

1 Caprice
5 Rung #1 of an apt word ladder
9 "Too frustrating for me!"
14 Michael who played the title role in 2014's "Cesar Chavez"
15 Melville work following "Typee"
16 Exploding stars
17 History moving forward
20 Bring up . . . or something brought up
21 Same-___ marriage
22 "Phooey"
23 Canine command
25 "The Amazing Spider-Man" director, amazingly enough
28 Trade show
30 Alternative to Target
32 Rung #2 of the ladder
34 Ire
38 Actress Falco
39 Supermarket section
40 Readily open to change
41 Snowy expanse
44 In a nervous manner
45 Lowest number not found on a grandfather clock
46 Woman's name that's a city in Oklahoma
47 Takes five
48 Rung #3 of the ladder
49 "And yet . . ."
50 Quench
52 Italian province where Moscato is produced
54 Follower of crack or crock
55 Shadow
58 Where Hawks soar: Abbr.
60 South side?
62 Cry when warmer weather returns
67 Taqueria option
68 Jai ___
69 Funny Samberg
70 Subscription option
71 Rung #4 of the ladder
72 Not nice

DOWN

1 Typist's stat: Abbr.
2 Experience auditory hallucinations
3 Latin phrase on memos
4 New World parrots
5 English head
6 Global financial org.
7 "Didn't intend for that!"
8 Irish girl's name related to the word "honor"
9 Dutch banking giant
10 Stuffed with ham and Swiss cheese
11 Allege
12 Big employer in Huntsville, Ala.
13 Try
18 Charlemagne's domain: Abbr.
19 Losing line in tic-tac-toe
23 Spit in the food?
24 I-, in chemistry
26 Gusted
27 City just east of Gulfport
29 1950s–'60s TV emcee Jack
31 Not be bothered by something
33 Lower limits, in math
35 National Zoo animal on loan from China
36 Current event?
37 Hindu's bindi, traditionally
39 Needing moisturizer
40 Gift for a ukulele player
42 To whom "Do You Want to Build a Snowman?" is sung
43 "It's mine!"
48 Deadly
49 Style of yoga in a heated room
51 Identify
53 Best

by Mary Lou Guizzo and Erik Agard

55 Peter or Paul
56 Area abutting a transept
57 Country with a Supreme Leader
59 ___ land
61 Part of a Viking message
63 "Uh-uh"
64 Singer/ songwriter Smith
65 One you might squabble with in the back seat
66 OB/___

53 ★ ★

ACROSS

1 Forest hatchling
6 Home of Hells Canyon and Heavens Gate Lookout: Abbr.
9 Root site
14 Chitchat
16 St. ___, only nation named for a woman
17 1968 Clint Eastwood western with six nooses on its poster
18 Much-trapped animal in wilderness America
19 It's hardly a Champagne cooler
20 "Why ___?"
21 Highest peak in N.Z.
22 "Sick, dude!"
23 Cheer at a Texas football game
26 Exclamation usually made in a high voice
29 Enemy agency in "Get Smart"
30 Cleaner brand with the slogan "Hasn't scratched yet!"
32 Dead spot
34 91, in old Rome
37 Toy boxer in a classic two-player game
40 Something much sold on St. Patrick's Day
41 PBS series since 1974
42 Some long sentences
43 Emcee's need
45 Be all thumbs?
46 "Show the world what you've got!"
52 Short-term job
54 Rob who directed "This Is Spinal Tap"
55 15-time N.B.A. All-Star Duncan
57 This, that or the other
58 Combine
59 "Hands in the air!" . . . or a literal hint to 17-, 23-, 37- and 46-Across
62 Tall, slender wineglass
63 Shapes of many car air fresheners
64 Like computer data, with "in"
65 London ___
66 Cheeky

DOWN

1 Fall color
2 "Some jerk he is!"
3 Cha cha slide, e.g.
4 Lang. of 16-Across
5 Counterfeiter trackers, in old lingo
6 "Does this seem fine to you?"
7 Jab
8 German cry
9 Dillydallier
10 Kitchen utensil brand
11 Best ___
12 Use for a bed
13 Partner of recreation
15 [Gulp!]
21 Eponymous hypnotist
24 Classic Scottish breakfast item
25 Nut
27 ___ Terr. (geographical designation until 1889)
28 "Ain't that the truth!"
30 Clothing item with hooks
31 Chemical variation
33 Champagne specification
34 Halo and Gears of War
35 Goes on
36 "___ a long story"
38 "Heroides" poet
39 Cosine of 0
44 Bolting down, say
46 Company that merged with Heinz in 2015
47 "Nervous" sort
48 Get ready for a Mr. Universe contest, say
49 Benjamin
50 Like computer data, with "in"
51 Danglers from rear-view mirrors

by Brian Thomas

53 Hit musical with the song "Everything's Coming Up Roses"

56 N.Y.S.E. and Nasdaq: Abbr.

59 Tanning fig.

60 Madre's hermano

61 1970s–'80s cause, for short

54 ★★

ACROSS

1 Metallic waste
6 Isn't a bystander
10 Longtime Syrian leader
15 Preferred seating request
16 Get ready for planting
17 In __ (developing)
18 Understood
19 Ithaca, to Odysseus
20 Odysseus, to Ithaca
21 Les __-Unis
22 Patent preceder
23 Girder type
24 Lineage-based women's grp.
25 "__ be my pleasure!"
27 "Star Trek: __" (syndicated series of the '80s–'90s)
29 Draft org.
30 Pizza chain
31 Stumblebum
33 Rare craps throws
36 Like Mercury among all the planets
41 Legendary Manhattan music club
45 "Here comes trouble!"
46 Distance for Captain Nemo
47 __ package
48 Big name in mortgages?
49 TV host Ryan
51 Singer Carly __ Jepsen
52 Hide away
54 Place to go to swim, informally
55 Mythical figure known for ribaldry
57 Writer Edgar __ Poe
59 Places where streams flow
60 Indirect comment . . . or a hint to this puzzle's circled letters
66 Org. for students in uniform
67 Danish money
68 Blackberrys, e.g., for short
69 Spread in a spread
70 27 Chopin works
71 Bombard
72 Acorn, essentially
73 Deals with
74 Indulged to excess, with "on"

DOWN

1 Like the slang "da bomb" and "tubular, man!"
2 Vaquero's item
3 Award for Washington and Lee
4 Pupil of a lizard, e.g.
5 Becomes established
6 Garden pest
7 Dummkopf
8 "Personally . . ."
9 Worry about, informally
10 The Charioteer constellation
11 Bit of theater detritus
12 Tennis Hall-of-Famer with a palindromic name
13 Arts and hard sciences, e.g.
14 Sides of some quads
26 Pictorial fabric
28 Studying aid
30 Grp. that gets the show on the road
32 Recipient of media complaints, for short
33 Some turkeys
34 [Yawn!]
35 1-1
37 Well-organized
38 Eponymous physicist Ernst
39 Horrid sort
40 Chop __
42 Made the rounds, say?
43 It varies from black to white
44 Ballpark purchase
49 N.B.A. Hall-of-Famer with four rap albums, informally
50 "The Tale of __ Saltan" (Rimsky-Korsakov opera)

by Jeffrey Wechsler

53 Like some golf shots and most bread

56 City under siege from 2012 to '16

58 "No __" (bumper sticker)

59 Page 2, 4 or 6, generally

60 Space balls

61 Art Deco notable

62 Dissolute man

63 Butts

64 "Dogs"

65 Abbr. on a brewery sign

55 ★ ★

ACROSS

1 Kept for a rainy day
9 Place where people are going with their drinks?
15 Norman Bates or his mother, in "Psycho"
16 Advice for relaxing
17 Top-level list
18 Judge appropriate
19 Ninny
20 One of the choices on a computer's 17-Across
22 Brown or blacken
23 Welcome at the front door
26 Get dressed (up)
27 Portable workstation
30 ___ it out (fights)
32 Chinua who wrote "Things Fall Apart"
33 Order in the court
34 Concert piece
37 "Here's something for you to think about, you ingrate!"
39 One who spreads discord
41 Shade provider in Thomas Gray's "Elegy Written in a Country Churchyard"
42 Coalition
44 Mindlessly
45 Request during a physical checkup
46 Beginning of many workdays
47 [I don't care]
50 Onetime division of the Chrysler Corporation
52 Sweatshirt part
53 Finding on Snopes.com
54 "Are you ___?"
57 "Ciao"
59 Manage to detach by hitting
63 Have a quick look-see, say
64 Language of the pre-Roman Empire
65 Some IHOP choices
66 Western villain . . . or a hint to four answers in this puzzle

DOWN

1 Spiritual guide
2 "___! 'tis true I have gone here and there" (start of a Shakespeare sonnet)
3 "That so?"
4 Place where plots are hatched
5 The radius runs along it
6 Small
7 Politico who called the press "nattering nabobs of negativism"
8 Incredulous question
9 Worst in a competition
10 Can
11 Animal that shares its name with a king of Thrace in the "Iliad"
12 Sights along the Champs-Élysées
13 Aid for a fugitive
14 Take another shot at
21 Habituate
23 Burgoo, e.g.
24 Kind of purse that sags
25 In public
26 "What are you waiting for?!"
27 Frilly
28 Long
29 "Close call!"
31 A geisha might be found in one
34 Shivering fit
35 Self-referential
36 Place for a king and queen
38 Overdo the flattery
40 Prefix with particle
43 Takedown piece
45 Numbers game

by Nancy Stark and Will Nediger

47 Where many cabins are found
48 Comfortable and welcoming
49 "Got it"
51 Will, more emphatically
53 Clothing department
54 Unpleasant find in a sweater
55 __-Pacific
56 Ding
58 Edge
60 Suggested qty.
61 Inc. alternative
62 Symbol of strength

56 ★ ★

ACROSS

1 What you might do if you skip a step
5 Like old-fashioned diapers
10 "Selma" director DuVernay
13 Four-star review
14 "Tiny Bubbles" crooner
15 Onetime ruler in the Winter Palace
16 *Insomniac's complaint
19 Japanese lunch box
20 Root beer brand
21 Half-___ (coffee option)
22 Alternative to Tide or Cheer
23 *Leaving dirty dishes on the counter, say
27 ___ cava
28 Firefighter tool
29 Limit
31 Part of a Swiss roll?
33 Ambulance figure, for short
34 Green stone
35 Rain heavily
36 *Sexy detective

38 Bay ___
39 Force on the ground
40 Abbr. in a criminal profile
41 Like the posts at the top of a blog, typically
43 Growling dog
44 Showy neckwear
45 Fifth book of the New Testament
46 *Works like an anti-aging serum
49 West Coaster's summer hrs.
52 Fed-up feeling
53 Certain library loan
54 Lessen, as fears
56 Liquid evidenced by the answers to this puzzle's starred clues?
60 Tiny bit
61 Off the table?
62 Part of N.B.
63 First word of many California city names
64 "___ Anatomy"
65 General ___ chicken

DOWN

1 Group making a reservation?
2 Go-kart, e.g.
3 Ex of the Donald
4 Confined, with "up"
5 Contents of jewel cases, for short
6 Nabokov novel
7 Last year before A.D.
8 1931 boxing movie for which Wallace Beery won a Best Actor Oscar
9 "___ on it!"
10 "Yeah, whatever"
11 With 12-Down, actress Joan whose last name consists of two different conveyances
12 See 11-Down
15 Contraction that starts "Jabberwocky"
17 Cat or top hat, in Monopoly
18 Oil crisis?
24 Completely jumbled

25 Wiped out
26 Ralph who wrote "Only the Super-Rich Can Save Us!"
27 Not stay the same
30 Split tidbit
31 Grounds for discussion?
32 Alliterative ice cream flavor
33 H, as in Athens
34 Highest-grossing film before "Star Wars"
35 ___-12 (N.C.A.A. conference)
37 "As you wish," to a spouse
42 Allen or Hawke
44 Rush-hour sound
45 Actress Hepburn
47 The Krusty ___ (SpongeBob SquarePants's workplace)
48 Egg-shaped
49 Bends at a barre
50 "Book 'em, ___!"
51 Rug rats
55 Rainbow flag initialism
56 Letters at a filling station?

by Erik Agard, Amanda Chung and Karl Ni

57 Org. with ties to Sinn Fein

58 Part for tuning a guitar

59 Connections

57 ☆ ☆

ACROSS

1 Happening after doors open on Black Friday
8 Draw
15 Colorful circles
16 Ronan of "Lady Bird"
17 1982 movie starring Julie Andrews
19 Elicited with difficulty
20 Some mortgage adjustments, in brief
23 Run, old-style
24 Skeletons in the closet, so to speak
28 To be, overseas
29 Tighten (up)
31 Money holder
32 Swimmer Ian who won three gold medals in the 2000 Olympics
34 Japanese floor mat
36 Helpful people to know
37 Warning sign
41 Triple ___
42 Collegiate basketball competition, for short
43 Like Natalie Portman, by birth
44 It ended during the Napoleonic Wars: Abbr.
45 Kind of switch
47 Label owned by Sony Music
48 Good earth
50 Formerly
51 Its second ed. contains about 59 million words
52 Miss the mark
53 1% alternative
55 Like many radios
57 A long way off
60 Common sign-off
61 Source of the word "kiwi"
62 River draining 11 countries
63 8:00-9:00 p.m. in prime time, e.g.
64 Deduce
65 Down in the dumps
66 Go down, in a way
67 Like many A.T.M.s
68 Primetime ___

DOWN

1 Western Conference player, informally
2 Shapiro of public radio
3 World AIDS Day mo.
4 More eccentric
5 Soothing succulents
6 1986 #1 Starship hit with the lyric "I'll never find another girl like you"
7 Third-person pronoun
8 Parenthesized comments
9 Food truck offering, maybe
10 Figure, as a sum
11 It may be read to the rowdy
12 Sheet music abbr.
13 Hit CBS series with three spinoffs
14 Spill the ___ (dish out gossip)
18 Line on a leaf
20 Holder of many cones
21 Like some cuisines
22 2008 movie starring Michael Sheen and Frank Langella
25 Movie with graphic violence . . . or what 17-Across, 22-Down or 39-Down each is?
26 Some board game equipment
27 Jazzes (up)
29 Souvenir shop purchases
30 List shortcut
33 Information on a ticket
35 Light on one's feet
38 "ER" role for Paul McCrane
39 1997 movie starring John Travolta and Nicolas Cage
40 Like many pipes nowadays
46 Knock down
49 Like butterscotch
53 Annual Austin festival, for short
54 ___ nut
55 Dictator deposed in 1979

by Christopher Adams

56 Swampland, e.g.
58 Many a
   university donor,
   informally
59 "Ratatouille" rat

58 ★ ★

ACROSS

1 Walk in big boots, say
6 Practically
10 Alternative to Venmo
14 A3s, A4s and A8s, in the automotive world
15 Black-and-white item you can consume whole
16 Adjoin
17 Like galoshes weather
18 Ground beef sandwich with Swiss cheese and caramelized onions
20 Success story like Uber or Airbnb
22 "True Detective" and "True Blood" airer
23 Poehler of "Parks and Recreation"
24 Institutions propped up with government support
30 When repeated, start of a cheer
33 Newton who lent his name to three laws of motion
34 "That's my ___!"
35 Da Vinci's "___ Lisa"
36 Catherine who married Henry VIII
37 Gives the cold shoulder
39 McGregor of the "Star Wars" prequels
40 "Just joshin'!"
41 Verb whose past tense is formed by moving the first letter to the end
42 Matrimonial path
43 Chinese path
44 One profiting through litigation, not innovation
47 Granola ___
48 Granola bit
49 Misconceptions about money . . . or a loose hint to 20-, 24- and 44-Across?
57 Discuss one's toilet habits, for example
58 West African republic
60 Something a complainer might raise
61 Easter basketful
62 404 Not Found, e.g.
63 Lodgings
64 Aussies with deep pockets?
65 Poke

DOWN

1 "Wheels"
2 Beach bash
3 Ruler of Valhalla
4 1" version of a 15-Across
5 Mind reader
6 "Didn't bother me at all"
7 1978–79 revolution site
8 Trips up
9 Provocative comments on current events
10 Toyota debut of 1982
11 Help the offense?
12 Classic George Takei role
13 Beginning of a link
19 Orange dish
21 Queen's honour, for short
24 "That's enough out of you!"
25 Universal Studios Japan site
26 Brother of video games
27 Balladeer
28 Less than right
29 Sister
30 "Why do you think that?"
31 Totally
32 Group of talking heads
35 Israel's Golda
37 Role in hide-and-seek
38 It's over your head
42 Chief law officer: Abbr.
44 "Ugh" reviews
45 To boot
46 Scot's headwear
47 Homes for owls
49 Hubs
50 Turgenev who wrote "Fathers and Sons"
51 Deutschland turndown
52 "Othello" schemer
53 Ship of myth
54 Drive-___ window

by Michael Hawkins

55 Like walnut shells

56 Smooch, in Britspeak

59 "___ we finished now?"

59 ★ ★

ACROSS

1 Volunteer's offer
5 Fivers
9 Nickname for Cleveland Browns fans
14 Talking in a movie theater, e.g.
15 Withered
16 World Golf Hall-of-Famer Lorena
17 Tome
20 Like Guinness
21 Dandies
22 Editorial override
23 Down Under predator
24 Unsavory sort
26 Court org. — or a former court org.
27 D.C. summer setting
28 Palindromic girl's name
30 Often
32 Bonny miss
34 Barely manage, with "out"
36 It's generally not played so much
37 Notable
41 Give a raw deal
44 Have a bug
45 Nashville landmark, familiarly
49 Goon
52 Goose egg
54 Issa of "Insecure"
55 Boston Garden legend Bobby
56 See 51-Down
58 They can carry a tune
60 Crime film genre
62 Noah Webster's alma mater
63 Star __
64 Request needed to understand four clues in this puzzle
67 Pass
68 One of Thanos's foes in the Avengers movies
69 Vet school subj.
70 It may have a big mouth
71 __ souci (carefree)
72 Popular bait for catching striped bass

DOWN

1 One who doesn't believe
2 Subject of Hemingway's "Death in the Afternoon"
3 Rubs oil on
4 Label on some packages of jerky
5 Pale wood
6 Sexy, muscular man
7 Gaffe
8 Oozed
9 Bobs and bouffants
10 Doesn't sit idly by
11 Common riddle ending
12 Spoiled
13 Tear-jerker
18 Cry of surprise
19 "Got it"
25 Banned pollutants
29 Frost relative
31 Childish retort
33 Nos. at the beach
35 Watergate-__
38 __ and Carla (1960s R&B duo)
39 Tina Fey's role on "30 Rock"
40 "The Book of __" (2010 film)
41 Cadged
42 Wonder Woman, for one
43 Big news regarding extraterrestrials
46 Barbecue griller's purchase
47 Moderate's opposite
48 "We totally should!"
50 Terrier type
51 Says "56-Across!," for example
53 Card count
57 Kind of shirt
59 Cocoon dwellers
61 Geom. figure

by Damon Gulczynski

60 ★ ★

ACROSS

1 Goof
4 Mexican resort area, for short
8 Car body option
13 Bets everything one's got
16 Bond wore a white one in "Goldfinger"
17 Commercial holiday mailing
18 Strands at a ski lodge, say
19 *Louis Pasteur, 1885
21 Losing poker player's declaration
24 U2 can call it home
25 *Roald Amundsen, 1906
33 Street cleaning day event
34 "Stat!"
35 Where Apia is found
36 Queens's Arthur __ Stadium
38 *William Herschel, 1781

42 Half of square dance participants, typically
43 One-named Latin singer
45 "I'll do that job"
47 Letter above a sleeping toon
48 *Howard Carter, 1922
53 Heart and __
54 Ver-r-ry small
55 Google returns . . . or the answers to the four starred clues
62 Partner of part
63 Enhances, as an original recording
67 Old British biplanes with an apt name
68 Home of the Titans
69 Pick on
70 Unwanted blanket
71 Chicken __

DOWN

1 Goose __
2 Reine's husband
3 One issuing red cards, for short
4 The "C" of F.C. Barcelona
5 Others, in a Latin list
6 Wait
7 Length of a quick tennis match
8 Favorable outcome
9 Prez or veep
10 Lucy's man
11 Deuce follower
12 Abstainer's portion
14 Peacock's walk
15 Annual mystery writer's award
16 Pageant topper
20 __ access
21 Still in one piece
22 Kind of pork on a Chinese menu
23 ". . . am I right?!"

26 Sch. system with campuses in Pullman and Spokane
27 Big part of an elephant
28 Aromatherapy spot
29 Droop
30 Seattle-based retail giant
31 Magic creatures of Jewish lore
32 Pass slowly and carefully
37 Time to remember
39 Bit of Oscar recognition, informally
40 French article
41 Something to confess at a confessional
44 Where it's happening
46 Kind of fly
49 Competitor of Target
50 "Ben-__"
51 Bells and whistles, maybe
52 Exams
55 Dust-up
56 Overhang

by Ross Trudeau

57 Verdi's "La donna è mobile," for one
58 Some HDTVs
59 Appear

60 "Let me think . . . huh-uh"
61 Helmut of fashion
64 Topic in parapsychology, for short

65 Vintage car inits.
66 Possible reason for an R rating

61

ACROSS
1 Showy accessories
5 Invitation stipulation
9 Goddess in a chariot pulled by peacocks
13 ___ Duncan, Obama education secretary
14 Place where beads are made
15 So-called universal donor type, for short
16 Saying suggesting that worldly possessions should be enjoyed
19 Beloved, in Bologna
20 Division of a hacienda
21 Actress Scala
22 Like Bill Clinton's presidency
25 Iconic introduction in cinema
27 Batman co-creator Bob
28 Longtime Mississippi politico Trent
31 Father of the American Cartoon
32 What one gets after many years of work
33 2008 political catchphrase
36 Instructor's remark after making a mistake
40 Like a sleeper cell?
41 Power ___
43 Head: Ger.
46 Actress Blanchett
47 "A forest bird never wants a ___": Ibsen
48 Insistent refusal
51 Agreed to, in a way
53 Part of some Hebrew men's names
54 Preceder of Edison
57 What goes above and beyond?
58 Where you go for a fresh start . . . or a hint for four answers in this puzzle
63 It's a two-hour drive north of Pittsburgh
64 Noggin
65 European capital
66 Tony and Emmy winner Tyne
67 Length
68 Give an appointment to

DOWN
1 Feature of Cajun Country
2 Goblinlike creature
3 Rain forest menace
4 House rules may not apply here
5 Bucolic call
6 Just for ___
7 ___ Day (supplement)
8 One way to get out of jail
9 The way
10 Puzzle
11 Adjusts, as laces
12 Dumbstruck
14 Like an overcast night sky
17 Number of sides on a triangolo
18 ___ Express (Delhi-to-Agra train)
22 Ring finish, briefly
23 "Where's ___ ?"
24 Common artwork in New York City subways
26 Fashion editor Wintour
29 First name in dance
30 Convictions
33 The dark side
34 One of a 1970s TV family
35 Court V.I.P.: Abbr.
37 Sleeper that never dreams
38 Quack remedy
39 Literary character who says "I will wear my heart upon my sleeve"
42 French politico Marine Le ___
43 Gnarly, as a tree trunk
44 Mark ___, 1998 P.G.A. Player of the Year
45 What a doodle might be in
47 Subs (for)
49 Man's nickname that sounds like a pest
50 Trying tasks
52 Nautical propeller

by Lewis Rothlein

55 Cognac age indicator
56 Cool shade
59 What makes a tumbler spin
60 Samovar
61 Doctors Without Borders or Oxfam, in brief
62 "Let's ___!"

62 ☆ ☆

ACROSS

1 A ewe for you, say
6 Mideast's Gulf of __
11 Swelling reducer
14 Popped up
15 Some bonds, for short
16 Yule drink
17 Was barely victorious, as in boxing
19 Brooklyn Brown or Newcastle Brown
20 Storage unit
21 Diplomacy
22 Hershey coconut bar
24 Mavens
26 Cole Porter song from "Kiss Me, Kate"
28 Not for kids, say
30 Acquires the film rights to
31 Target numbers
34 Saturn S.U.V.

35 Baseball rarities nowadays . . . or a phonetic hint to the starts of 17-, 26-, 48- and 57-Across
39 __-lacto-vegetarian
40 More blue
41 Ones who never listen to oldies?
44 Big name in oil
48 As something different to do
51 Mediterranean tourist attraction
52 Bo's'n's quarters
53 Oil or kerosene
55 Bit of work
56 Swear words?
57 Opposite of "consumed daintily"
60 Stephen of "V for Vendetta"
61 Tender spots

62 How many times a clock's little hand goes around in a full day
63 Strongman player on "The A-Team"
64 Not quite a strike
65 Possessed

DOWN

1 Where to order oysters
2 Beethoven's Third
3 Lift : elevator :: __ : car hood
4 Mil. morale booster
5 On its way
6 Gas brand with a torch in its logo
7 World capital at 9,350 feet
8 "Commonwealth" novelist Patchett
9 Computer image file format

10 Put into categories
11 60 minutes from now
12 Brewskis
13 Casts out
18 Do beat work
23 Everything, with "the"
25 Forest giants
27 Given medicine
29 Do some voice work
32 Actress Thompson
33 "Caught ya!"
35 Often-naive reformer
36 Garment left in a cloakroom
37 Magazine with an Agency of the Year award
38 "Zip-a-__-Doo-Dah"
41 Validate
42 High-end Mercedes line
43 Lonely place, so they say

by Alan Arbesfeld

45 Substitute (for)
46 How curry dishes are often served
47 Pestered
49 A Lion, but not a Tiger, informally
50 External appearance
54 Jared of "Dallas Buyers Club"
58 __ of Good Feelings
59 "So cute!"

63

★ ★

ACROSS

1 Demanding
6 Who said "A woman's perfume tells more about her than her handwriting"
10 Croque-monsieur ingredient
13 ___ View (streaming site)
14 "Dies ___"
15 Beer purchase
16 Kind of alcohol
17 "The Twits" author
18 Nike rival
19 Ornately decorated money?
22 Perfervid
25 Snowcapped, say
26 March meant to end a drought?
30 Oven handle?
31 Adamant refusal
32 Mistake indicator
35 Yellow card displayers
36 Lists of commands
37 Building site code?
38 AC/DC single with the lyric "Watch me explode"
39 Israeli president who was the author of 11 books
40 Commotion
41 Bumper version of a cart?
44 Fireplace receptacle
46 Beginnings
47 What the trees by Walden Pond provided?
51 Frequently cosplayed sci-fi character
52 Socially aware
53 Yellowish color
57 Bend over backward
58 Some
59 Member of an early 20th-century French art movement
60 Pick up
61 [Been there, done that]
62 Let go

DOWN

1 A word before you go
2 ___ milk
3 "I'm trying to work here"
4 Vegan source of protein
5 Four-time Grammy-winning gospel singer Adams
6 Mischievous trick
7 Modern locale of ancient Sumer
8 Home to Interstates H-1, H-2 and H-3
9 Takes a refresher course in
10 Plan (for)
11 Like some elephants
12 George ___, general at the Battle of Chancellorsville
15 Wrist bones
20 Way on Waze: Abbr.
21 Sheep's cry
22 Not with the group
23 Noodle soup
24 New addition to the team
27 Guy in a restaurant
28 Didn't just rent
29 Galvanize
33 "Could you turn on the A.C.?"
34 Weapons for the X-Man Wolverine
36 Dissolve
37 It was once drawn on the street
39 Ballet move
40 Quarterback's option
42 She played Mrs. Which in 2018's "A Wrinkle in Time"
43 What might have a crush on you?
44 America's first ICBM
45 ___ Khan, tiger in "The Jungle Book"

by Brendan Emmett Quigley

48 Tucson school, informally
49 Twist
50 Cut
54 Strawberry or peach
55 She was tempted
56 Visibly ashamed

64 ⭐ ⭐

ACROSS

1 Veronica ___, author of the best-selling "Divergent" series
5 Green and soft, say
10 Movie with famous "dun dun" theme music
14 Measurement that might be a lot?
15 Some Japanese cartoons
17 Profess
18 Menu item #1: A bowlful of Cap'n Crunch that's been on top of the fridge for four years
20 Rhyming opposite of break
21 Officers-to-be
22 Opera term that's sometimes a woman's name
24 Coffee alternative
25 Austin Powers or Jack Bauer
26 Menu item #2: The charred remains of a slice of whole wheat
29 W.C.
30 "___ Flux" (1990s sci-fi series)
32 Kinds
33 Org. whose participants wear helmets
35 Follower of Mary
37 Zip
38 Plea concerning the menu in 18-, 26-, 53- and 64-Across?
42 Chest coverer
43 "Eight more hours and I'm outta here!"
44 "Ya got that right"
46 Subject of a sleep lab study
49 Words to a backstabber
51 Go out for a bit
53 Menu item #3: A Red Delicious, assuming you find sawdust delicious
57 Writing surface
59 Wrath
60 Fail to enunciate
61 Cow sans calf
62 Ben ___, pirate in "Treasure Island"
64 Menu item #4: Something to pour in coffee for a sour surprise
67 "Stat!"
68 Pig, cutely
69 Dot on an ocean map
70 Future-gazer
71 City in West Yorkshire
72 N.B.A.'s Young, familiarly

DOWN

1 Troublemaker
2 Stop sign shape
3 Sacrifice of square footage for location, e.g.
4 ___ Keller, first deaf and blind person to earn a Bachelor of Arts
5 PC alternatives
6 "He still the ___" (lyric in Beyoncé's "Countdown")
7 Word before and after yes, in the military
8 Below-the-belt campaign tactic
9 Long (for)
10 Song one loves, in modern slang
11 Image next to a user name
12 Most socially conscious
13 Comfy pants
16 Not much light can get through it
19 Grammy-winning James
23 Bewildered
26 Wild hog
27 Not satisfied, as expectations
28 "___-daisy!"
31 Actor Idris
34 Media lawyer's specialty
36 Roll with a hole
37 Sound of failure
39 Broken bone revealers
40 Toy for a windy day
41 Ingredient in a melt
45 Kneecap
46 Close chicas
47 Read over
48 Dance done to the 2015 hit "Watch Me"
50 Not new
52 Started listening, with "up"

by Alison Ohringer and Erik Agard

54 As well
55 It gets bigger in the dark
56 Accident-___
58 The sky, perhaps
61 That woman's
63 Broadcaster of "Wait Wait . . . Don't Tell Me!"
65 1950s prez
66 Guided

65 ★ ★

ACROSS

1 Head on a plate?
8 Bloviating type
14 Egg-shaped
15 Worth mentioning
16 Global scare
18 Place to go off track?
19 Speak at a level pitch
20 In accordance with
22 King's College of Our Lady of ___ Beside Windsor
23 Image formed by connecting this puzzle's circled letters from A to N and then back to A
27 Lust, but not love
28 Sportscaster in the documentary "Telling It Like It Is"
29 Ref. work begun by the London Philological Society
31 One taking care of the bill

32 Pool parties?
35 Modern line at an airport
38 Towel provider, often
40 "You got it!"
41 French bakery offering
43 Strand during a ski trip, say
45 Major seller of health supplements
46 Peace in the Middle East
48 Keepers of the records?
51 Where a 17-Down becomes a 23-Across
54 Same-sex union?
55 Branch of yoga
56 French bakery offering
58 Diamond pattern
61 Chief in the Creek War of 1813–14
63 Dormmate
64 People whose political views are "Communist lite"
65 Anago, at a Japanese restaurant
66 Has in mind

DOWN

1 Duplicates
2 "Forward!," in Florence
3 Fashionable society
4 Raise one's hand for, say
5 Port north of the Horn of Africa
6 Hand-held console introduced in 1989
7 Teacher of Samuel
8 John and Mark, for two
9 Following
10 Wolf (down)
11 It's always cut short
12 Part of NATO: Abbr.
13 Thousand bucks
17 One that becomes a 51-Across
21 Home of the Rams before 2016: Abbr.
24 Paper clips have lots of them
25 Past the baseline, in tennis
26 Michelle of "Crazy Rich Asians"

28 Spanish word repeated in a welcoming phrase
30 Something to fall back from: Abbr.
31 Air traveler's convenience, informally
33 In good shape
34 A in German 101?
35 Boot brand from Australia
36 En ___ (with all of a court's judges)
37 Engrave
39 Smoothie flavor
42 Its N.Y.S.E. ticker symbol is "X"
44 Entered carefully
47 Comment from a hot bath
48 Sight in a Chinese parade
49 Like Nelson Mandela for 27 years
50 Underline, say
52 Pay for play
53 Bulldog
54 Fail to show up as expected
57 Euro division
58 Married couple?
59 Sushi garnish

by Alex Eaton-Salners

60 Indian state whose largest city is Vasco da Gama

62 Lead-in to center

66 ★ ★

ACROSS

1 Make known to customs officials
8 Makes a decision on Tinder
14 Sending out a memo, say
16 Mother ___
17 *1956 sci-fi movie with Robby the Robot
19 Big name in classic video games
20 Undergo a chemical change
21 Self-referential
22 *2006 rom-com starring Amanda Bynes and Channing Tatum
27 Curvy letter
28 "Bien sûr!"
29 Obama ___
30 Put 10,000 hours into, it's said
33 Forgets to include
35 *1961 musical for which Rita Moreno won an Oscar
38 "Wouldn't that be nice!"
39 Word often repeated with a different pronunciation
40 ___-Manuel Miranda, creator of "Hamilton"
41 Texter's qualifier
42 British P.M. beginning in 2016
45 *1953 musical with songs by Cole Porter
51 Tucker out
52 Fabulous writer?
53 Parts of the spine
54 What the film answering each starred clue was inspired by
59 Gay of the New Journalism movement
60 Rush of Black Friday shoppers, e.g.
61 Wearable by anyone
62 "I'm laughing so much it hurts!"

DOWN

1 Slander
2 Hams it up on stage
3 Ring figures
4 Large scale of the universe?
5 Et ___ (citation words)
6 Relieved (of)
7 Finish
8 Legendary snake exterminator, for short
9 Actress Raquel
10 Mad as hell
11 Write down
12 Linguistic suffix
13 Took a load off
15 Actor Richard
18 Classic game console, for short
22 Figure (out)
23 "Play that beat!"
24 Only female Israeli prime minister
25 Like many modern black-and-white films
26 Lil ___ X, rapper with the 2019 #1 hit "Old Town Road"
28 Bit of salty language
30 Some advanced degs.
31 Tokyo's former name
32 Cancel, as a fine
33 "Beetle Bailey" dog
34 Herd noise
35 Conflict with the European Theater of Operations, for short
36 German one
37 "Me too!"
38 Category
42 Gave the wrong message
43 Business whose income is computed quarterly?
44 "But of course!"
46 "For goodness' ___!"
47 Reagan attorney general
48 County name in England and five U.S. states
49 Keystone character
50 "Great" creatures
51 Actress Hedren
53 Pelosi and Schumer, informally
54 Fox News commentator Varney, familiarly
55 China's ___ dynasty

by Evan Mahnken

56 Ring figure
57 You can bank on it
58 Unit of sunshine

67 ★★★

ACROSS

1 Biased investigation
10 Showing shock
15 Hospital sign
16 Total
17 What the British call a station wagon
18 Parting words
19 Laura of "Star Wars: The Last Jedi"
20 Hot dogs
22 Positions
24 Charlotte ___, capital of the U.S. Virgin Islands
25 Iraq War danger, for short
26 Sellers at a craft show
28 Symbol of strength
31 Taunts
32 Twice, musically
33 Some baseball stats
34 Foreshadowed
35 Well-known speaker
36 Boomer baby
37 Charlatan
38 Smarts
39 Some marbles
41 Word on all U.S. coins
42 Show allegiance
43 Upscale kennels
47 Author much used by other authors
50 Word after who, what or anything
51 Get ___ of reality
52 Mid-19th-century czar
54 Robert who played filmdom's Mr. Chips
55 Yosemite attraction
56 Long-running pop culture show
57 Pointing of fingers

DOWN

1 Policy details, metaphorically
2 "No more for me, thank you"
3 Prefix with fluoride
4 Narrow openings
5 6 ft., maybe
6 Followed
7 Last of the Mohicans
8 Member of the C.S.A.
9 Part of a 17-Across
10 Sister of Apollo
11 Sources of jam, jelly and juice
12 Union-busting, say
13 Like the 1930s Soviet Union
14 Has
21 Stale
23 Disney collectible
26 Right hands
27 KOA customer
28 Portmanteau for lovers
29 Trampled
30 Brown family member
31 Complete embarrassment
34 Pharmacy brand
35 Commissioner inducted into the Baseball Hall of Fame in 2017
37 Uncovers, with "out"
38 Monopolize
40 Vacillate
41 Police commissioner Gordon's turf
43 Bing Crosby's record label
44 Montana motto word
45 Silk center of India
46 Subject for Raoul Dufy and Henri Matisse
48 Spoiler of a perfect report card

by Randolph Ross

49 Breathing aid
53 Unseal, in
poetry

68 ★★★

ACROSS

1 Toilet paper?
9 Having many openings
14 Powerful Russian
15 Fancy affair
16 Coca-Cola product since 2001
17 Cafe chain
18 "O.G. Original Gangster" rapper
19 Overly sentimental writers
21 Junípero ___, founder of San Francisco
23 Arizona athlete, for short
24 Media co. led by the Sulzberger family
25 Events with tents
27 Really bugged
29 Airer of Neil deGrasse Tyson's "StarTalk"
30 Become edible
34 Kind of coordination
36 Be charged
37 Touristy area on the Irish coast
39 Wiccan groups
40 Balkan capital
41 Things held in a cannonball
42 Place to watch a race, for short
45 Tony once nominated for an Emmy
47 ___ May Lester of Erskine Caldwell's "Tobacco Road"
49 Vitamin-rich green side dish
52 Setback
53 ___ center
54 Popular vodka brand from Holland
56 Front spoiler on a car
57 Like many people on January 1
58 Fancified
59 Spaces out

DOWN

1 Pueblo Revolt participants
2 1930–'40s film star with the signature song "You'll Never Know"
3 Unshackles
4 Cause associated with the rainbow flag
5 ___ Americana
6 Newspaper section
7 Provincetown catch
8 Weekly Jewish observance
9 Request for backup?
10 Isn't bad?
11 Fancify oneself
12 Commodore in Sondheim's "Pacific Overtures"
13 Passover no-no
15 Thyme keeper?
20 Suddenly took notice
22 Feature in a telephone directory
26 Any man or boy, biblically
28 Collection of posts about a trip
29 Part of 24-Across
31 Million-selling 1977 Donna Summer song
32 Many a British retiree
33 Some tech grads, for short
35 Sombrero, e.g.
38 Ethnic group whose name means "wanderers"
42 The planets, e.g.
43 Gateway of a Shinto shrine
44 Get on
46 Fox Islands resident
48 They have big mouths

by Sam Ezersky and Byron Walden

50 Spiral-horned antelope

51 Italian source of smoke

55 ___ salad

69

⭐ ⭐ ⭐

ACROSS

1 "No, really"
8 Sort
15 Carpet cleaner
16 High-minded sort?
17 Give a flat fee?
18 Back in the stadium
19 [Can you believe they wrote this?!]
21 TV commentator Navarro
22 Abbr. in math class
23 Stock at a wine bar
27 Off the wall
30 Battle of Soissons setting
32 Place for a miniature flag
33 Goon
34 Weapon with a rope and balls
35 Literary nickname for Dolores
36 One of the Smithsonian buildings
39 What "they" can only be, to grammar sticklers
40 Enliven, with "up"
41 Signal
42 Iowa town where Grant Wood's "American Gothic" is set
43 Shade of red
44 Word with chicken or news
45 Go here and there
46 Tight spot
47 Scare quote?
49 Pitch to a publisher
55 Paper that runs mots croisés
58 Seeing someone, say
59 When Caesar says "Yond Cassius has a lean and hungry look"
60 Prized sheep
61 1831 Poe work
62 Prizes

DOWN

1 Carnival Cruise stop
2 Twosome
3 ___ tide
4 Walk alluringly
5 "Well . . ."
6 Aspires to do something
7 "Star Trek: T.N.G." role
8 Mount near Haifa
9 Like a squashed circle
10 Peugeot symbol
11 It may come long after the play
12 Gangbusters, for short?
13 "___ soon?"
14 Go astray
20 Exercise started by crouching
24 Per
25 Not stray
26 Did phenomenally onstage
27 Debugging tool?
28 Cyclops killer of myth
29 Poet who wrote "Tonight I can write the saddest lines"
31 Ayaan Hirsi ___, Somali-born advocate for women's rights and religious freedom
32 Online hilarity
34 Healthful breakfast choice
35 Do-nothing
37 Ska band instrument
38 Be garrulous
43 Make hand over fist
44 Epicure
46 "Doctor Who" actress Whittaker
48 Good genre for a maze maker
50 Intro to Torts student
51 "The Bicycle Thief" setting
52 All together, so to speak
53 Bond collector?
54 Not so great
55 W.W. II craft: Abbr.

by Brendan Emmett Quigley

56 Pro-sustainability, in lingo

57 "It doesn't excite me"

70

ACROSS

1 Player in a baseball stadium
6 Kind of system in which 64 is 100
11 "Hold on ___!"
14 "Serial" podcast host Sarah
16 "Far out!"
18 ___ Panza, sidekick of Don Quixote
19 Not go out to dinner
20 ← ÷ 40
22 Jesus, with "the"
23 Went to bat (for)
25 Adjective on Tex-Mex menus
26 "Seriez" is a form of it
28 Things with microgrooves
29 Winner of the 2016 Pulitzer Prize for Drama
38 Almost certainly
39 Backdrop to AMC's "The Walking Dead"
40 Remote area?
41 Letters on some bulletproof vests
42 Mass-produce, with "out"
45 Big name in mops
50 One of a kind
54 Beer pong receptacle
56 Seemingly expressing
58 Wife in F. Scott Fitzgerald's "Tender Is the Night"
59 Fugitive's destination, maybe
60 Painter's undercoat
61 Sly chuckle
62 Newspaper divisions
63 Group of near nobodies

DOWN

1 "Your point being . . . ?"
2 Mounts with a little white on top?
3 French novelist/dramatist associated with the Theater of the Absurd
4 Dried chili pepper on Tex-Mex menus
5 Greeting in Guangzhou
6 Fall behind
7 Scorch
8 Home to Rodin's "The Kiss," with "the"
9 Slightly
10 When Taurus begins
11 Oenophile's criterion
12 Copied
13 Word with space or rock
15 British writing award
17 Region near Mount Olympus
21 Bauhaus-influenced typeface
24 Hospital sections, for short
27 Nudges
28 Celebratory round
29 Tracy and Jenna's boss on "30 Rock"
30 Odysseus' rescuer
31 Marvel series depicting the Tet Offensive, with "The"
32 Annual June sports event, informally
33 Cut off
34 Colorful birds
35 Bite
36 Letters that come before AA?
37 House call?
42 Not stay awake any longer
43 "Manners require time, as nothing is more vulgar than ___": Ralph Waldo Emerson
44 ___ the Hittite, soldier in King David's army
46 Popped (out)
47 Main

by Finn Vigeland

48 C.D.C. concern
49 Game sheet
51 Burrowing animal
52 Pompeii's Temple of ___

53 Made, as a putt
55 Fresh
57 Shortest Magic 8 Ball response

71

ACROSS

1 Sci-fi character who graduated from Starfleet Academy in 2359
5 What Iran and Iraq do
9 "Purgatorio" poet
14 Brownie, for one
16 Primitive kind of poker?
17 Dangerous cocktail
18 "__ fine"
19 Luxury hotel option
21 Name related to Rex
22 Wednesday, e.g.
24 Insurance company whose logo contains a bill
27 Tudor house feature
30 Vegan protein source
31 Pot-making supply
32 Like a mythical lion
33 Recipe directive
34 Put away the dishes?
35 Memorable White House Corres-pondents' Dinner host of 2006
36 You might click it open
37 "Eww, stop!"
38 Singular thing
39 Requiring immediate attention
40 Hebrew : ben :: Arabic : __
41 "Stop playing" symbols
42 Optimistic
43 Strained, at the bar
45 Dash device
46 Creamy, fruity drink
53 One who's frequently in the dark
54 Fiancée, say
55 Brief bridge opening
56 Like privates, often
57 Part of a pound?
58 Recipe directive
59 Cameos and others

DOWN

1 1/256 of a gal.
2 Plastic Clue weapon
3 Strong team
4 Cube holder
5 South __, N.J.
6 Boy with a bouquet
7 Surfing destinations
8 Something to spin
9 One who's 60-something?
10 One with a plant-based diet
11 Spotless
12 London museum whose oldest piece is from 1900
13 Some TV drama settings
15 Provisional
20 Sensitive figure, for many
23 Most populous city in Oceania
24 __ acid (dressing ingredient)
25 Attention-grabbing
26 Epitome of romantic passion
27 Fixes
28 Bounds
29 Natural food coloring sources
32 Rejection of a honey-do list
35 Its ribs stick out
39 Cleaning cloth
42 Wind or unwind
44 It was boosted by Atlas
45 Cloddish sort, in slang
47 Things waiters wait for
48 Huff

by David Steinberg

49 Long dress
50 "I ___ quotation": Emerson
51 Amazon unit
52 James B. ___, diving bell inventor
53 Secant's reciprocal: Abbr.

72

ACROSS

1 Sport with stunt riding, informally
4 "Heck if I know"
9 Big difference
14 Axe product
16 Goes on and on
17 Reflective stretch
18 Item checked at an airport
19 Misses overseas
20 Gone
21 Trio in a children's rhyme
22 Three-lobed design
25 Roughly 37% of U.S. immigrants
28 Personal bearing
29 Jung ___, author of the 1991 best seller "Wild Swans"
30 It's generally up and running within a few hours
31 "Breaking Bad" protagonist
32 Lead-in to sat

33 Aquarium performer
36 Like a happening party, in slang
37 Olympic Australis, for one
39 Suffix with Jumbo
40 North Carolina home of Appalachian State University
42 Brand with the slogan "Fill your glass"
44 What makes a possum play possum
45 A-number-one
46 Fifth-brightest star in the night sky
47 Part of a pod
48 Author who wrote "Show me a woman who doesn't feel guilty and I'll show you a man"
53 "The Cocktail Party" dramatist
54 Model company?

55 Book in which the Israelites are rebuked for idolatry
56 Common board requirement, in brief
57 Vamooses
58 Winner of nine Grand Slam tournaments in the 1990s
59 Components of many free apps

DOWN

1 Summer outdoor events, informally
2 Manifestation of sulkiness
3 Chose at the ballot box
4 Almost nothing on?
5 Public perception
6 Worn-out
7 2Pac's "Dear ___"
8 Result of prolonged screen time, maybe
9 "Golly!"
10 Threw some back

11 Celery sticks topped with peanut butter and raisins
12 Fixed cord for a paratrooper
13 One source of the umami taste
15 Title figure in a Gilbert and Sullivan opera
23 Quick move?
24 Word with fan or form
25 Come right up to
26 One who always has time to spend?
27 2007 satirical best seller
28 Tops in athletics
30 Professional feeders
34 Constantly updating GPS figs.
35 Widely followed court battles
38 You might experiment with this on
41 Bingeing
43 Ends
44 Crack, in a way
46 Like some very important signs

by Peter Wentz

49 Carny's target
50 Plant also known as ladies' fingers
51 Grant consideration
52 E.T.S. offerings
53 Middle of summer?

73

★ ★ ★

ACROSS

1 Matchmaking services?
8 Co-star of "The Office" who played Ryan Howard
15 In a classic form of diamond
16 Victor's gloating cry
17 Rust
18 Technophobe
19 They may be fluid: Abbr.
20 Banished
22 Smidgen
23 Shepherd's pie ingredients
25 Venture a view
26 Miss
27 Radiates
29 "No ___ can live forever": Martin Luther King Jr.
30 Street hustler's game
31 Many a corny pun
33 Bravado
35 Lord Tennyson's "The Eagle," e.g.
36 Shaker's cry?
37 Speed of sound
41 Baker's shortcut
45 Certain Bedouin
46 Aladdin's simian sidekick
48 Looks
49 Defeats by a hair
50 Dumps
52 Auto parts giant
53 "The enemy of ___ is the absence of limitations": Orson Welles
54 Vehicle used by the police to catch thieves
56 "Delta of Venus" author
57 Mob law?
59 Like many screenplays
61 "The Call of ___" (short story by H. P. Lovecraft)
62 Creamy Italian dish
63 Colorful display in a weather report
64 Places in the field

DOWN

1 Slumped
2 Cream in a cobalt blue jar
3 "Once again . . ."
4 Trailblazed
5 Four-letter fruit pronounced in three syllables
6 "Au contraire . . ."
7 The point of church above all?
8 Ghostwriters lack them
9 Unit of energy
10 Like Rodin's "The Thinker"
11 Dated
12 Rendering useless
13 Phoenician goddess of fertility
14 Snack company that's a subsidiary of Kellogg's
21 Top part of a face
24 Capital of Newfoundland and Labrador
26 Reduce one's carbon footprint
28 Copycat's comment
30 Targets
32 Comprehension
34 Ring letters
37 One referred to as "the crown"
38 "You all agree with me, yes?," in one word
39 Modern screen test
40 Savor the praise
41 Stage holdup?
42 Had it in mind
43 Sacrilege
44 Tic-tac-toe plays
47 Smidgen

by Trenton Charlson

50 ___ Baron Cohen, player of Borat

51 Title woman of a Beatles song

54 Lip ___

55 Scrape

58 Published

60 Party person, for short

74 ★★★

ACROSS

1 Blogs, social media and other nontraditional outlets
12 Enlightened responses
15 Option when changing jobs
16 ___ Irvin, early cartoonist/designer for The New Yorker
17 Dirt spreader
18 Roam (about)
19 Winter Olympics sights
20 Italian sculptor ___ Lorenzo Bernini
21 Section of a Crayola box
22 ___ talk
23 Campaign supporters
24 ___ Park
25 Words of explanation
27 Pennsylvania city where the Delaware and Lehigh Rivers meet
28 Exhibiting a modern form of obsession
31 Quick way to end a sentence?
32 "Where does it all end?" argument
33 Socket for setting a gem
34 Food preservers
35 "Any ___?"
36 Dolphinfish, informally
38 Flavor additive, in brief
41 It goes clockwise or counter-clockwise depending on the hemisphere
42 Legend says it arose on Palatine Hill
43 Search for prey
45 ___-con
46 Offshore waves?
48 Grade of wine
49 Projecting beams on a bridge
50 Cornerstone abbr.
51 Reading and writing, for most jobs

DOWN

1 Guinness Book adjective
2 "Go, me!"
3 Of renown
4 Stepped
5 Start of a start of a menu?
6 The Liberty Tree, for one
7 Ad agency specialist
8 Picker-upper
9 Fuel for planes
10 Follower of four or six, but not five
11 Mess up
12 Containing silver
13 Without deliberation
14 Breakup tune
21 Forwards
23 Little squealer
24 Hollande's successor as president of France
25 Factor in Billboard rankings
26 Buster of myths
27 Latin list ender
28 Extricated from a jam
29 Reason
30 Concept of beauty
31 Slow and steady types
32 Prestigious academic journal
36 When cock-a-doodle-doos are done
37 Italian known for pulling strings?
38 Paradigm
39 Ice cream choice
40 Part of a makeup kit
42 Org. fighting copyright infringement
43 Like very early education, for short

by John Guzzetta

44 ___ Shankar, influence on George Harrison

46 Chemical contaminant, for short

47 High ways?

75 ★ ★ ★

ACROSS

1 Hosp. units
4 ___ peas
10 Basics
14 Kind of flour
15 1965 Michael Caine spy thriller, with "The"
17 ___ grano salis
18 What might help a hacker go undetected?
19 Deride
21 Kentucky's northernmost county
22 Abbr. in an auction catalog
23 Gambling card game
24 "Doctor Faustus" novelist
25 Part of an oven
27 Similar (to)
28 Actor with seven Primetime Emmys
30 Greek cheese
31 Tennis player, to sportswriters
33 Op-ed, e.g.

35 Cocktail with rye whiskey
37 Sean Hannity and Chris Hayes
41 Quarry of cartoondom's Gargamel
43 Pope when Elizabeth I took the throne
44 Virus in 2003 news
47 Cellphone component
49 Do some programming
50 Stud of the sports world?
52 Walked over
53 Hard ___
54 Footwear brand since 1978
55 Hollywood agent Michael
57 Military gathering?
58 Journalist's tool since '67
61 Home of Sen. Mike Crapo: Abbr.
62 Political leader?

63 Sister
64 Elate
65 Like baking dough
66 Big mean on campus

DOWN

1 Those who've seen both Europe and Asia, say
2 Home to Lake Waiau
3 1928 Winter Olympics site
4 Keeper of the flame?
5 Mil. address
6 Dives with a tank
7 W.W. I battle locale
8 "Give it to me straight"
9 Jacket letters
10 Behind, at sea
11 "Kiss my grits!"
12 You're not in it if you're out
13 Car model originally called the Sunny in Japan
16 Tallow source

20 Rosina Almaviva, in "Le Nozze di Figaro"
24 Go pirating
26 "Unless it's impossible"
29 Got back (to), in a way
32 "Uhhh . . ."
34 "Eureka!"
36 Review
38 Programming manager's specialty
39 Did a bit of cleaning
40 Only daughter of Joseph Stalin
42 Typeface that shares its name with the Roman goddess of luck
44 Marks on shoes
45 Who said "Take it from me, every vote counts"
46 The Midwest or the South
48 More than half of scores

by Rachel Maddow and Joe DiPietro

76 ★ ★ ★

ACROSS

1 Display, as an image, using only a small number of different tones
10 Goes on
15 Way out in space
16 Enlightened sort
17 "Further . . ."
18 Site of a 1974 fight won by 40-Across
19 Ron ___, nine-time All-Star from the 1960s–'70s Cubs
20 Kid with a moving life story?
22 "The Wire" stickup man
25 Become completely absorbed
26 G.I. garb, for short
29 Strike out on one's own
32 Staples competitor starting in 1988
34 Swell

39 Put away
40 See 18-Across
41 Many a private investigator
42 Try
43 Hot take?
45 Like many shorelines
47 Car lot designation
48 Philosopher who said "A journey of a thousand miles must begin with a single step"
52 Puzzle (out)
54 "We're done here"
57 "Enough!"
61 Restraint
62 1983 #1 hit with the lyric "Take, take, take what you need"
65 Co-star with Shatner and Nimoy
66 So-called "Father of Zoology"
67 Cinemax competitor
68 Common business attire

DOWN

1 Bible supporters, often
2 Org. with inspectors
3 Good look
4 One who might needle you?
5 With 59-Down, spa supply
6 Band with the monster album "Monster"
7 Market event, briefly
8 Novelist ___ Neale Hurston
9 Linda of Broadway's "Jekyll & Hyde"
10 Slugabed
11 Ishmael's people
12 Ending with Oxford or Cambridge
13 Gogol's "___ Bulba"
14 Correction corrections
21 Chem. unit
23 Questionnaire info
24 Parmesan alternative

26 ___ analysis
27 Men's grooming brand
28 Dramatists' degs.
30 "Gesundheit!"
31 Lime and others
33 Popular cracker topper
35 "How rude!"
36 Crackerjack
37 Shade
38 Piece of punditry
44 Email address ending
46 1921 play for which the word "robot" was invented
48 Airs
49 Plagued
50 City at the mouth of the Yodo River
51 Real stunner
53 Improvises, in a way
55 [Can't wait!]
56 Brief researcher, briefly
58 Riesling alternative, familiarly

by Damon Gulczynski

59 See 5-Down
60 Intel satellites, metaphorically
63 Dark side
64 High-speed inits.

77 ★ ★ ★

ACROSS

1 Group in the original "Ocean's 11"
8 Classic arcade game with lots of shooting
14 Like Istanbul
16 Emphatic admission
17 First world capital, alphabetically
18 Like clothes buttons, generally
19 Unexciting poker holding
20 2008 Bond girl Kurylenko
22 Bedevil
23 Car once promoted with the line "The thrill starts with the grille"
25 Speaker units
27 Prefix with -gon
28 Nocturnal acronym
29 Strange things
32 Super 8, e.g.
33 Group of female seals
34 Powerhouse in Olympic weightlifting
36 Gradually
39 Animated character who graduated from Dogwarts University
40 The "R" of 28-Across
41 Circular parts
42 Formidable opponents
44 Campaign aid
47 "The Old Curiosity Shop" girl
49 Touched
50 Rail center?
52 Express stress, in a way
54 Gulf of ___
56 Santa ___, Calif.
57 Juiced (up)
59 Jacob's partner in "A Christmas Carol"
61 City nicknamed "The Old Pueblo"
62 So-so, as support
63 Acropolis figure
64 Spots

DOWN

1 One going against the grain?
2 Poem greeting the dawn
3 "What's past is past," e.g.
4 Giant competitor
5 Last name of cosmetics giant Mary Kay
6 "See ya"
7 Bad way to go
8 Buffalo's home: Abbr.
9 Has-___
10 Source of stone used to build the ancient Egyptian pyramids
11 Flag-waving and such
12 Musical "girl who cain't say no"
13 Joe known as "The Comeback Kid"
15 Cause of bad dreams, in modern lingo
21 Follower of bon or mon
24 Show immediately preceding another
26 Scuffle
30 For adults only
31 Special-education challenge
33 Bottom line?
35 Tom Sawyer's half brother
36 Request for food delivery
37 Someone who's pretty darn good
38 It could be on the tip of your tongue
39 ___ rap
43 More, in México
44 O.C.D. fighter, maybe
45 Put forth

by Neville Fogarty and Doug Peterson

46 Enamors
48 Small slip
51 "___ done now?"
53 Superbright
55 "The Wizard of Oz" farmhand
58 Helicases split it
60 Court divider

78

ACROSS

1 Pilot control?
7 For all to see
13 What "e" may signify
14 Bonnie of "Parenthood"
15 Occasion for a piñata
16 Couldn't say "say," say
17 Gathering clouds and others
18 Poker site
19 Glued to something
20 Sluggers
21 Ortiz of "Devious Maids"
22 Yoga command
23 Island dish
26 Opposite of downs
28 Arrangements of teeth?
30 Freak
32 Modern test subject
33 Shade of gray
34 Bygone skating spectacle
37 "Aunt" of a 1979 best seller
38 Org. concerned with cracking and leaking
39 He wrote "It is always by way of pain one arrives at pleasure"
40 Cooler
41 Goes out in the rain
42 Babysit
43 Dr. Lester portrayer in "Being John Malkovich"
46 One of the 12 tribes of Israel
47 Successful Olympic bidder
48 Ravel work in which the melody is passed among the instruments
49 Ones prepared to drop a few bucks?
50 Tanning salon fixture
51 "Weird . . ."
52 Noah and Wallace of old films

DOWN

1 Ride around the block, say
2 Warner Bros. cartoon series of the 1990s
3 Breath-taking experience
4 Quaint retort
5 Line at a food stand?
6 Snow ___
7 Provided new hands
8 Common airport kiosk gadgets
9 Giveaways
10 "Grace Before Meat" essayist
11 Virtually every coin
12 Goggle
14 "Jeannie Out of the Bottle" memoirist
16 Like some bad pitches, in baseball lingo
18 Office building, equipment, etc.
20 Canine command
23 Spot for a stud
24 Rambo, e.g.
25 Changes keys?
27 Canine command
29 Took in
31 In rhythm
35 Iago vis-à-vis Jafar, in "Aladdin"
36 Decided
41 Bugged
42 Common material in tutus
43 "What a surprise to see you here!"

by Ryan McCarty

44 Cream
45 Hacking targets, for short
46 "By __!"
48 Mac alternative

79

ACROSS

1 Pot component
5 "Calm down, ace"
9 Saved
13 Successor to Paar's successor
14 Partner of 5-Across
15 Full of ups and downs
16 Everyone included, after "to"
17 Attends to some personal care
19 Pulitzer winner for "Sunday in the Park With George"
21 Captivate
22 Bug expert?
23 Boarding pass info, for short
24 Celestial beast
25 Cheese made from goat's milk
27 Puts the pedal to the metal

31 Hepatologist's study
32 Product introduced in 1984 with an ad titled "1984"
33 Restaurant cook on TV's "2 Broke Girls"
34 2017 recipient of the Presidential Medal of Freedom
35 Actor Cronyn
36 Port authority?
38 It gets you from station to station
39 Talked too much
40 Cousin of a corset
41 Yard sale caveat
42 "Just like that!"
43 Three-ingredient sandwich
44 Largest moon of Pluto
47 The Weeping Prophet

49 Zombies
51 Parisian being
52 Billy the Kid, for one
53 Kind of speculation
54 Parent
55 Indication of pain or pleasure
56 Carriage
57 Durango direction

DOWN

1 School card
2 Genetic disorder carried by Queen Victoria
3 "Regardless . . ."
4 Where you might hear someone say "Duck!"
5 Worn out
6 Mitchum rival
7 Look like
8 "You rang?"
9 Character in "Camelot" and "Monty Python and the Holy Grail"

10 Fictional queen of Arendelle
11 Commercial pitch
12 eHarmony info
15 Big Bird attended his memorial
18 Narc's concern
20 Mozart title
24 Sore spot
26 Menu heading
27 Not as bright
28 Media-friendly audio clips
29 "Something's not right here . . ."
30 Words of consolation
32 Press conference sights
34 Revealing
37 Accelerator particles
38 Marathoner's focus
40 Make a bed?
42 Memphis blues street

by Robyn Weintraub

44 Silent sort
45 It has views of Mauna Loa and Mauna Kea
46 Asics competitor
47 Force-ful one?
48 Only
50 Murky

80 ★★★

ACROSS
1 Official on a Segway, maybe
8 Rotating part of a tape recorder
15 Merchant with tiny shopping carts
16 Another name for an ear shell
17 Epitome of completeness
18 Edits, as text
19 When el Día de los Reyes is celebrated
20 It's an honor
22 Playground declaration
23 Edward Fairfax ___, "Billy Budd" captain
24 Exclaimed
26 Little sweater?
27 Back
28 Changed course quickly, at sea
30 Christmas bowlful
31 1992 hit for k.d. lang
34 Reddish orange
35 Radio format for Radiohead
41 Chit in a pot
42 Heavy-handed administrations
43 De : French :: ___ : German
44 Big Caribbean exports
46 Massenet opera
47 ___ Belbenoît, noted escapee from Devil's Island
48 Jazz genre
50 Web portal with a Bing search bar
51 Sickos
52 Court order
54 Conforms (to)
56 Ignore the alarm, say
57 Downtime
58 Heartfelt
59 Depot's terminus?

DOWN
1 One role for a helicopter
2 Simultaneously
3 In a bit
4 Petrol measure
5 Role for Liz in '63
6 Subj. of the 2003 book "The Meaning of Everything"
7 Reason to refuse an invitation
8 Those prone to recidivism
9 White House nickname
10 Puppet
11 Single-masted boat
12 Trattoria dessert
13 Keeper of logs?
14 Savings
21 Nutrition science
24 Band selection
25 Obtained (from)
28 Edwin with the 1970 #1 hit "War"
29 Dwellers on the North Sea
32 Abbr. in an office address
33 See, in Tijuana
35 Where drones return
36 Parsons of old Hollywood gossip
37 Lock component
38 Inundate
39 Persuaded one
40 Mideast diet
45 Philosopher Kierkegaard
47 Dodgers Hall-of-Famer whose #1 has been retired
49 Word with organ or cleaner
51 Man's nickname in a metropolitan orchestra?
53 Member of the family, for short

by Roland Huget

55 "Ad majorem
___ gloriam"
(motto of the
Jesuits)

81

ACROSS

1 Island nation with a cross on its flag
6 Series installments, for short
9 Unit of energy: Abbr.
13 Had, as food
14 Secure
16 ssorcA-41?
17 Edwin of 1960s–'70s R&B
18 Cop's station in England
20 Sweet farewell
22 Given to picking fights
23 States of confusion
24 Part of the English translation of "Notre Dame"
25 Part of Act 4 of "Antony and Cleopatra" in which Antony attempts suicide
28 Islamic spirit
31 Things rested on, metaphorically
32 Bollywood actress Mukerji
33 Scottish John
34 Agricultural commune
37 How a package may arrive
38 Lady in Arthurian legend
40 One with a big mouth in Africa?
41 Corporate giant named for a mountain
43 Make some definite plans
45 "Interesting . . ."
46 Spares, maybe
47 Dishonest sort
50 Beauty lesson
54 One for whom a flash in the pan is a good thing
55 Title woman of a classic 1928 André Breton novel
56 Ronald Reagan ___ Medical Center
57 Where bills pile up
58 Trap until it gets warmer, say
59 Grey Goose competitor
60 8-bit game console released in 1985
61 Wait on

DOWN

1 Hide
2 Web developer?
3 Something a shepherd may have on
4 Twisting effect
5 Alternative music subgenre
6 Like some tanks and promises
7 "Oh, baloney!"
8 One and only
9 Ice cream holder
10 Precisely
11 Monitors
12 ___ bike
15 Superlative for a cake
19 Jackie of "Rush Hour"
21 Letters associated with WNYC and KQED
25 Shade of black
26 Mötley ___
27 "Livin' La ___ Loca"
28 Is mortified, so to speak
29 Transgender rights activist and best-selling author of "Redefining Realness"
30 At the outset
31 End piece?
35 Dressed up, maybe
36 Crease smoothers?
39 Trying time
42 Warmly welcome
44 Judge
45 Search engine result
47 Rolls up
48 Where to get down from?
49 One of the Gandhis

by Erik Agard

51 Titular professor in a Nabokov novel

52 Rhyming prefix with novela

53 "Stay in your ___"

54 Gloomy one

82

★ ★ ★

ACROSS

1 Text ___
6 No bull market?
15 Mr. or Mrs. Right?
16 Like some sodas
17 "Another Suitcase in Another Hall" musical
18 Little Orphan Annie feature
19 Concern of "three strikes" laws
21 Hollow
22 Home to Dyess Air Force base
23 Avian epithet for Napoleon II, with "the"
25 Certain flu vaccine medium
28 Echo preceder
29 Mob pieces
30 Cleaves
32 And many times in France?
33 Has a fit, maybe?
34 Queen ___

37 Class for an English major, familiarly
38 Home of Triple-A baseball's Aces
39 Only poisonous snake in Britain
42 Coffee-growing region of Hawaii
44 Ones hanging around a haunted house?
46 Street sweep?
47 Golden rice and others, in brief
48 Sitcom mother portrayer of 1987–97 and (on a different show) 2002–05
51 Hides who one is
53 Ocho preceder
54 Achieved green efficiency?
55 Like some monologues

56 FedEx Office competitor
57 Places in brackets

DOWN

1 Toy package info
2 Old TV show set on the Pacific Princess, with "The"
3 Homer and others
4 Fixes, as a shower stall
5 Masonry and others
6 Know-it-all, in Britspeak
7 Powerful car engine
8 Sorts frequently given detention
9 Terse denial
10 "___ regrets?"
11 Haulers on runners
12 Mobile greeting
13 To fix this you need to get cracking!

14 Coin whose name means "small weight"
20 To some extent
24 City where, according to legend, Cain and Abel are buried
26 "Don't be ___" (words of caution)
27 "Darn tootin'"
31 Pre-cell?
33 Begin to give out
34 Rhyming nickname for wrestling Hall-of-Famer Okerlund
35 Booted out
36 Paintbrushes for applying spots and blotches
37 Ferdinand de ___, developer of the Suez Canal
38 "Use it or lose it" sloganeer
39 Whites
40 D, on a cornerstone

by Byron Walden

41 Mulligan
43 Black currant liqueur
45 Relative of a stingray
49 ___ Oper (historic concert hall in Frankfurt, Germany)
50 Even
52 "How's it hangin'?"

83 ★★★

ACROSS

1 Egg warmer
9 A rutabaga is a cross between a cabbage and this
15 Pavarotti standard whose name means "My Sunshine"
16 "No bet," in poker
17 "Ain't that somethin'!"
18 Doctor's wear
19 "Your Love Is King" singer, 1984
20 Stupid
22 Toshiba competitor
24 "God created ___ so that Americans would learn geography" (line attributed to Mark Twain)
25 With the bow, in music
27 Like many Christmas traditions
29 Some of Lockheed Martin's business
31 ___ chain
32 Committed
33 Like some jacket hoods
34 "100 Years . . . 100 Movies" org.
35 "And I get dumped on again"
38 Ubiquitous Chinese character
39 Like a three-pitch inning
40 Low-lying areas
41 Jerk
42 School cafeteria food, stereotypically
43 Stupid
44 ___ tide
46 D.O.J. branch
47 Chicago airport code
48 Businesses often near beaches
51 Spike
55 For three: Fr.
56 Backspin producer?
58 Style setter?
59 High-profile merger, e.g.
60 Riles
61 Plant from another country

DOWN

1 Does some diamond cutting?
2 Offshore
3 Jell-O maker
4 Like some reactions
5 Safe place to crash
6 "Your work inspires me"
7 Italian poetic form
8 "I won't be back till late"
9 Strict, demanding parent
10 Most-applied-to school in the U.S.
11 Hit 1970s sitcom
12 "Works every time"
13 Summer drink with caffeine
14 Tie-breaking shots in soccer: Abbr.
21 Refuse to drop
23 Nikon competitors
26 Cousins of Drama Desk Awards
27 "Enough!"
28 Terror in Arthur Conan Doyle's "The Lost World"
30 Tom of old late-night TV
32 "Jeez, that's a shame!"
33 Preceder of first
36 Common ingredient in baked beans
37 Ethel Mertz, on "I Love Lucy"
43 Just what the doctor ordered
45 Essayist's writing
49 It may pack a punch
50 Hammer's end
52 Choppers
53 Thunderous sound
54 Slithery

by Sam Trabucco

55 Asia's ___
Darya River
57 Broadside,
maybe

84 ★★★

ACROSS

1 Insects of the species Myrmica rubra
8 Kitchen scrubbers
15 "What are my other choices? There are none"
16 Food flavorer that's not supposed to be eaten
17 Try to hit with
18 "My treat"
19 Most crosstown thoroughfares in Manhattan . . . with a hint to this puzzle's theme
21 ___ Daily News (paper since 1878)
22 Employers of masseurs
25 Jeweler's creation
29 Start of some futuristic toy names
33 Short while?
34 Fed
35 With 41-Across, proceeding willy-nilly
38 Awakening
40 Subject for immigration legislation
41 See 35-Across
43 Back on the job?
44 Hang time, to a snowboarder
45 Like plays about plays, say
46 Physicist's proposal
47 Headdress decoration
49 Sparkle
52 Nightmarish Manhattan traffic situation . . . or a possible title for this puzzle
60 Progress
62 Access, as a computer network
63 Place of danger
64 Yogurt topping
65 Goes against a proposal
66 Chamomile alternative

DOWN

1 Johnny nicknamed "The Godfather of Rhythm and Blues"
2 Comparison word
3 Actor McGregor
4 Profess
5 Started to cry, with "up"
6 ___ alcohol
7 Lady ___, first female member of the British Parliament
8 Yanks' foes
9 Woman with a title
10 Artist with the 7x platinum album "A Day Without Rain"
11 Emulates Lady Macbeth
12 Small coffee cups
13 Morsel a horse'll eat
14 Provisos
20 Banks on a runway
23 Holden's younger sister in "The Catcher in the Rye"
24 Slow and stately compositions
25 Aquafina competitor
26 Realm of Queen Lucy the Valiant
27 Private ship cabins
28 Needle case
30 "___ idea!"
31 Frequent tweeter
32 The "I" of Constantine I?
35 Fancy collar material
36 Poker giveaway
37 Turkey club?
39 Peaks: Abbr.
42 Tolled
46 What bicyclists might ride in
48 Hooch

by Kevin G. Der

50 Ancient shopping place
51 Reading unit
53 ___ law
54 Part of A.D.
55 Bridal wear
56 Bank annoyance
57 Rush-rush
58 Pepsi, e.g.
59 Kind of vaccine
60 Honey ___ (Post cereal)
61 Get into

85 ★★★

ACROSS

1 Someone who cares too much?
17 Serious competition
18 It sends waves through waves
19 College Board offering, for short
20 Guarded
21 Nincompoop
22 Age
24 Foggy condition
27 They go to the dogs
29 Unrelenting
34 Stops streaming
35 Part of ISIL
36 Small slice of pizza?
37 Party hearty
38 X
39 Help in a gym
40 Poetic preposition
41 Draconian
42 Ex-Expo Rusty
43 Deliveries in the early 1940s
45 Hardly generous
46 Santa __
47 They have strong teeth
48 Salinger title girl
51 Prey for an eagle or bear
54 Monster of TV
57 Sophomoric rejoinder
61 1958 Bobby Freeman hit covered by the Beach Boys and the Ramones
62 Be beneficial to

DOWN

1 Part of a locker
2 Love symbol that names another love symbol if you move the first letter to the end
3 Moon buggy
4 Kick-start
5 Banned pollutant, for short
6 A large quantity
7 Show vanity, in a way
8 Have a large quantity of liquor
9 __'acte
10 Drink after a race, say
11 Pressure meas.
12 French toast maker, maybe
13 14-line poem with only two rhymes
14 Prefix with sperm
15 "No __"
16 Veteran's opposite
23 Certain letter addendum, for short
25 Result of an oil surplus
26 25-Down unit
27 Thread holder
28 Santa __
29 Word from the French for "mixed"
30 Civil rights icon Medgar
31 Quick way through a toll plaza
32 Summer Olympics host before Barcelona
33 Save for later
35 Giant
38 Eugene in labor history
39 Gives a blank look
41 __ Jorge (one of the Azores)
42 "He who holds the __ must be master of the empire": Cicero
44 Native of NW France
45 Kind of acting
47 Spirit
48 Some sked predictions
49 Completely ruined
50 Itzamna worshipers
52 Requested service
53 Palindromic man's name
55 It's flaky
56 Had too much, in brief

by David Steinberg

58 Dijon-to-Lyon direction

59 Teens fight, for short

60 Story assigners, in brief

86 ★★★

ACROSS

1 Nestlé product first sold in 1961
11 Leader among the Axis powers
15 Classic deli order
16 Shortly after
17 Corona with tequila and fruit juice, e.g.
18 Actress Campbell
19 Jeannette ___, first U.S. congress-woman
20 Country formed by a 1964 merger
22 John of the Plymouth Colony
23 Big rigs
24 #2
26 Staircase element
29 Goaltending spot
32 CB radio emergency channel
33 ___ society
34 "Count me out!"
36 Headline on a neighborhood poster
37 Article of apparel not originating where its name would suggest
38 Fancify
39 "The Ship" composer, 2016
40 Small firecracker
41 Redden, in a way
43 Spin like a gyroscope
45 Nouvelle ___
49 Annual June sports event
51 Style
52 Headache for Ranger Smith
53 Transcribed
55 One of the d'Urbervilles in "Tess of the d'Urbervilles"
56 Track at Universal Studios and the like
57 Pull a con on
58 "You shouldn't rely on me"

DOWN

1 "The Jungle Book" beast
2 Jermaine ___, six-time N.B.A. All-Star of the early 2000s
3 Real enthusiast
4 Split
5 Fire department ID
6 2001 Israel Prize winner
7 Ding, e.g.
8 Cause trouble
9 Condition caused by abnormal calcium levels
10 Part of a savanna herd
11 Classic diner order
12 Prepares for a drill?
13 Bon ___
14 Suited to serve
21 Early example of reductio ad absurdum
23 Fix a flat for?
25 Piazza dei Miracoli locale
27 Kind of collar
28 Block maker
29 Dangerous currents
30 Where dinars buy dinners
31 They're flipped at diners
33 Come down in buckets
35 Things that can't be loaded
36 Sends in a high arc
38 Janitor's item
41 Go straight
42 End . . . or start
44 Scenery features in a Road Runner cartoon
46 "Hundo"
47 Lumberjack at work
48 Bond villain ___ Stavro Blofeld

by Mark Diehl

87 ★★★

ACROSS

1 One talking a blue streak?
7 Get used to it
13 Segregated
15 Images on a timeline of human evolution, maybe
16 Keeps in reserve
18 Actors Aidan and Anthony
19 "Help yourself, there's plenty left!"
20 High points?
21 Layout with little concern for privacy
22 Poker challenge
23 Place for soldiers to eat
24 Paso __, Calif.
25 Agile African animals
27 "In what sense?"
31 Wasn't productive
32 Wine-tasting offer
34 Northern
35 Many a YouTube video upload
42 Not abundant
43 Spiny fish named after a bird
44 Babysat
45 Kind of development
46 OPEC nation since 2007
47 Render undrinkable, as alcohol
48 Ronda __, mixed martial arts standout of the 2010s
49 Seedy establishment
50 Rough Riders' rides
51 Precepts

DOWN

1 Made-to-order
2 Begin to remove, as a diaper
3 Defeats decisively, in slang
4 Some urban noise pollution
5 Not obligated
6 Do some cobbling work on
7 With 12-Down, blue cheese and black coffee, typically
8 Intro to a big announcement
9 Serious, as an offense
10 Loose, in a way, as planks or siding
11 Nasal spray targets
12 See 7-Down
14 Dodge S.U.V.s
17 Prefix with -gram
26 Like many coats with liners
27 Scold at length
28 Emergency room case
29 Acted evasively
30 Good times for shopping sprees
32 "Heaven forbid!"
33 [Boo-hoo!]
34 Rigel and Spica
36 Deserve something through hard work
37 Piece of armor worn over the shin

by Joe Krozel

38 Secure

39 Drip source

40 Give the eye

41 1985 novel

"___ Game"

88 ★ ★ ★

ACROSS

1 Tabs are kept on them
9 Managed to acquire
15 "Non-G.M.O." or "Dolphin-safe"
16 Muse symbolized by a globe and compass
17 Serve
18 Nag
19 Small phone charger type
20 Waiting for an answer, perhaps
21 Rafts
22 2016 World Series celebrant
24 Patriarch on "Game of Thrones"
25 D.C.'s D or C
26 Grandson of Esau
30 "Red" or "White" tree
32 Like some laps and raps
34 Half a rack
37 Pub fixture
38 "Is this for real?"
42 "Red" or "white" tree

43 Collaborator with Sedaka and Cooke on the 1964 album "3 Great Guys"
44 Writer who called New York City "Baghdad-on-the-Subway"
46 Some shot
49 "Not only that . . ."
51 Similar examples
52 Departure announcement
55 Ottoman ruler referenced in "The Count of Monte Cristo"
57 Fashion
58 Malfeasant
59 Hank who voices Moe Szyslak
60 "This way!"
61 Touch
62 Play stoppers

DOWN

1 Salt
2 One-eighth set, in statistics
3 Part of a London web address

4 Reason to check one's phone
5 Robinson ___, many-time Yankees and Mariners All-Star
6 Shanghai
7 Browse the web
8 Baby pool?
9 Personal interest, metaphorically
10 Oakland's Oracle ___
11 Expressions of affection
12 Prefix with -dermal
13 Jessica of "The Book of Love"
14 Ending with brick or stock
23 "Capisce?"
25 Working arrangement, for short
27 Conductor of science experiments on TV
28 Lead-in to a chef's name
29 P.R. concern

31 Departure announcement
33 Kill it
34 Much-debated inits. in 2010s politics
35 Vote in un parlement
36 Shields, tear gas, etc.
39 Hip-hop radio/TV host Charlamagne ___ God
40 Go on and on about
41 Opposite of free
45 Used performance-enhancing substances, in slang
47 Group of notes reflecting a five-sharp scale
48 Market purchases
50 Let loose?
51 Comic ___ Baron Cohen
52 Provider of protective coverage
53 Minestrone soup ingredient

by Sam Ezersky

54 Who said "How sharper than a serpent's tooth it is to have a thankless child!"

56 Paris's ___ Monceau

89 ★ ★ ★

ACROSS

1 Gum-producing plant
5 Addition to a compost pile
9 Rush home?
13 Store discount come-on
15 ___-Turkish War (post-W.W. I conflict)
16 "Doesn't concern me"
17 Take two
18 "Not true!"
19 Former Houston hockey team
20 Illustration, for example: Abbr.
21 Ad time filler, for short
22 Half of an interrogation team
24 Neighbors of Estonians
26 First American film in which a toilet is heard being flushed (1960)
28 Equally distant
31 Cry at a surprise birthday party
33 Shut (up)
34 Pull a fast one on
35 Chill
36 Where a stud might go
37 Big name in Deco design
38 Hipsteresque, in a way
39 Struck out
40 Like bonds designated AAA
42 A-listers
44 Little mischief-makers
46 Fernando or Felipe, once
47 Word with nursing or training
50 Touch of color
51 One making a living by pushing drugs, informally
54 Contend
55 Sound evidence?
56 Good earth
57 Stay with a friend, say
58 Concerning
59 What areology is the study of
60 Synthetic fiber, for short

DOWN

1 Sources of cashmere
2 Openly confident
3 ___ fusion (cuisine)
4 Large quantity
5 Like the role of Albus Dumbledore after the second Harry Potter movie
6 All huffy
7 "Me neither"
8 Poindexter
9 Gives away to a better home, in a modern coinage
10 Back in again
11 One who hates heights
12 Messes around (with)
14 Daffy Duck, notably
15 Addressees of valedictories
23 High point
24 "Nobody ever told me," e.g.
25 Deposits in some banks
27 Bit of punditry
28 "___ Death," movement from "Peer Gynt"
29 Metal in a junk heap
30 Cause of typos, humorously
32 One who gives a lot of orders
35 Be highly regarded
39 Clean lightly, as a floor
41 Listings in a travel guide
43 Metaphor for penthouse suites
45 Back problem

by Freddie Cheng

47 "Project Runway" cable channel

48 Turn back

49 Mimic's skill

50 Anklebones

52 Activity for which you need a fair amount of wiggle room

53 On

ACROSS

1 "No, thanks"
6 Rapper's release
10 Activity that might elicit stares, for short
13 Singer/actress Janelle
14 Theater option
15 Couleur du chocolat
16 "___ Ever" (Elvis song from "G.I. Blues")
17 Yamaha purchase
19 Hazmat regulator
20 USA competitor
21 Construction piece that describes what happens when you compliment me?
22 Kashyyyk denizen, in sci-fi
24 Contents of some sleeves
26 Olympic runner?
27 Up and a little to the left, for short
28 One who might be diagnosed with a polysomnogram

31 Cellist with a Presidential Medal of Freedom
32 Like some legal judgments
33 Singer seen annually on David Letterman's Christmas show
34 "Say no more - I'm on it"
35 "___ Mañanitas" (traditional Mexican birthday song)
38 GPS suggestion: Abbr.
39 Walletful
40 Aid in breaking down doors
42 Go down, so to speak
44 ___ South, div. of the 55-Acrosses
45 Pixy ___
46 #2 image among smartphone users?
49 Not straight up
50 "That's my cue!"
51 Taqueria order, informally
52 ___ Park, Calif.

53 "C'mon, man," in a syllable
54 Wetlands feature
55 See 44-Across

DOWN

1 "Count me in"
2 One of the nine weapons in 2008's expanded version of Clue
3 "That, in spades!"
4 See 8-Down
5 Lead-in to cow, horse or dog
6 Footwear with a tree logo
7 Who said "The Lord will roar from Zion, and utter his voice from Jerusalem"
8 With 4-Down, someone who might repossess your car when you go bankrupt?
9 Prefix with thermic
10 Like some vestments
11 1980s presidential candidate
12 Weak

15 So-so bond rating
18 Conquers
20 English breakfast, for example
23 "Ninotchka" actress, 1939
24 Mayoralty, e.g.
25 Close . . . but not THAT close
29 Unseeded?
30 Trim
31 French homophone of 30-Down
32 Stand-up comedian with the 2005 double-platinum album "Retaliation"
33 Companies known for their net profit
34 "Enough already!"
35 Many a Univision viewer, in modern usage
36 Armpit
37 Poet with the 1967 Pulitzer-winning volume "Live or Die"
41 Big name in parfum

by Erik Agard

43 Original airer of "Everybody Hates Chris"
44 Cracked
47 ___ Resorts International
48 "Je pense que ___" ("I think so": Fr.)
49 Tsp. or tbsp.

91

ACROSS

1 Means of interstellar travel
10 Supreme Court colleague of Ruth and Neil
15 Oklahoma tribe originally from the Southeast
16 Parts of nerve cells
17 An anchor is at its end
18 Five-time winner of FIFA's player of the year award
19 Sport __
20 Loser
22 Garners
23 What might hurt a celebrity's Q Score
26 Top of Scotland
28 Main
29 Word with Pacific or basketball
31 Sheep's milk product
32 Arm muscle, informally
33 "This isn't over"
36 Advice column query
37 Some facial treatments
38 Ad __
39 Forty-niners' equipment
40 First show to win 50 Emmys, in brief
41 Sister company of Century 21
42 Delta Air Lines hub in the Mountain time zone, for short
43 State capital known as the Cherry City
47 Great-great-great-great-great-great-grandfather of Noah
49 This clue's number divided by this clue's answer
53 Cells joined by other cells
54 Alternative to tea leaves
56 Modern information analyst
59 Who sings "Some Enchanted Evening" in "South Pacific"
60 Shortly
61 Kind of cup
62 Travels like the fly in sci-fi's "The Fly"

DOWN

1 Cancel
2 Letter found between two vowels in the alphabet
3 Felt off
4 __ Dome (former Indianapolis venue)
5 Something on the horizon
6 Like a rock and many a roll
7 Part of Caesar's boast
8 Something to set or pick up
9 Make nice to in a manipulative way
10 "The Lord of the Rings" role
11 Farm team
12 Certain facial piercings
13 Like the sound of surround sound, typically
14 "Again . . ."
21 Much of military history
24 Competition at Pebble Beach
25 Meat cuts that are often barbecued
27 Valkyries, e.g.
30 Drinks made from agave
31 Tricks
33 Hit 1999 film that popularized a slo-mo effect known as "bullet time"
34 Took a gamble
35 Nabisco brand
36 Question asked after opening one's eyes and blinking repeatedly
37 Like cockatoos and iguanas
44 Unlikely partygoer
45 Party, e.g.

by Evan Kalish

46 Selling points
48 Colorful Hindu festival
50 One providing directions
51 Abbr. after a series of 52-Downs
52 See 51-Down
55 Driving aid
57 Its head is usually at the bottom
58 "If u ask me . . ."

92

★ ★ ★

ACROSS

1 "Right?": Fr.
10 Org. whose founders include Cecil B. DeMille
15 Leading man?
16 Sturdy floor wood
17 Potent Hawaiian weed
18 Unsettled feeling
19 High-society people may put them on when in public
20 Alternative to a Lambo
21 A man or a mouse
22 Demolition letters
23 Not so far away
25 It multiplies by dividing
26 "Narcissus and Goldmund" novelist
28 ___ truck
30 Part of a guess in Battleship
31 Only place in the U.S. to host both the Summer and Winter Olympics, informally
34 Vacation souvenir, perhaps
36 Parent company of Pine-Sol
38 Blanket
39 Home of Millennium Park, informally
40 Sharing many of the characteristics of
41 Background noise
42 ___ boy
44 Goods, slangily
48 2019 #1 album by Tyler, the Creator
50 Medicine cabinet glass
53 "Brilliant!"
54 200-milligram units
56 Snow of "Game of Thrones"
57 Bibliographer's abbr.
58 Still around
59 1963 Four Seasons hit
61 Paintings of Adam and Eve, typically
62 Alternative to Kickstarter
63 Bond, e.g.
64 Fully fixed

DOWN

1 Jet popular in the 1960s and '70s
2 Flight attendant in "Airplane!"
3 Periods of growth
4 "Who is ___?"
5 Harsh cry
6 Expressive characters
7 Rough up, in a way
8 Come down (on)
9 Match
10 Boy's name that becomes a girl's name if you move the first letter to the end
11 Tricks
12 Steakhouse selection
13 Not have an accomplice
14 "You want to?"
21 Occult
23 Learn indirectly
24 Taken in
27 Orkneyan or Shetlander
29 Part of a cloverleaf
32 Pixelated, perhaps
33 "Nope"
35 Family hand-me-down?
36 Quickly drink
37 Long car trip?
39 Woman who has traveled to el Norte, maybe

by David Steinberg

43 Music style that might feature an accordion and a bajo sexto

45 G.I. meal

46 Put some juice into

47 Bless

49 Shade of black

51 Zillow listing

52 Ruined

55 Challenge

57 Fragile projectiles

59 Short smoke

60 House support

93

★ ★ ★

ACROSS

1 Like sauvignon blanc and pinot grigio, typically
4 Scrubber
9 Warrior pose in yoga, e.g.
14 Kiss cam displayer
16 Meg who wrote "The Princess Diaries"
17 What's found above a tilde
18 Orange half of an iconic duo
19 Smart set?
20 Things sandals lack
21 Firing locale
22 Repaid
25 Managed
28 Swindling trick
29 Shake off
30 Sapped of resources
31 % on the back of a baseball card, say
32 Get in the end
33 Disturbed states
36 Comic actor Barinholtz

37 Las Vegas casino with a musical name
39 Bites harmlessly
40 Two-time Grand Slam champion of the 1960s
42 Is sure to succeed
44 Some fishing attire
45 Hearty breakfast dish that includes potatoes
46 Pilot production?
47 ___ Games, company behind Fortnite
48 Battleship row
53 One-named singer with the 1993 platinum album "Debut"
54 "Nothing can stop me now!"
55 Mascot of the Winnipeg Jets
56 Pearl Harbor or Norfolk

57 Pulitzer-winning writer of "The Optimist's Daughter"
58 Leslie ___, main role on "Parks and Recreation"
59 Handful

DOWN

1 Spun wax, say
2 Trick
3 Org. offering athletic memberships
4 Very uneven
5 Title tenor role
6 Big name in pest control
7 The other side
8 "Who wants to step up?"
9 Unbeatable blackjack pair
10 Garments worn at beach parties
11 Type least likely to turn up in a hospital
12 New Year's Eve party freebie
13 "I already ___"
15 Caromed

23 Middle of a Latin trio
24 Puts off
25 Shark, to swimmers
26 Everyman
27 All available options?
28 Use smear tactics on
30 Rosy shade of makeup
34 What team leaders must frequently manage
35 Player of the Skipper on "Gilligan's Island"
38 Quite eager
41 Gather on the surface, chemically
43 Underling
44 BBQ restaurant handout
46 Mormon settlement of 1849
49 Country that has approximately 0% arable land

by Peter Wentz

50 Idle
51 Instead
52 Whole bunch
53 Company that makes the Mini

94 ★★★

ACROSS

1 Junk dealers?
9 Ghost buster, of a sort
15 Fix without doctoring
16 Many a magnet has one
17 Thought accompanying a light bulb
18 Like speakeasies and fridges, at times
19 One may be copped
20 "Bandleader" with a 1967 #1 album
22 Dr. ___
24 On the ___
25 Go with the wind?
27 '
28 Big times
30 Man's name that's an alphabet run
31 The Panthers of the A.C.C.
32 Commonplace
33 Passes, slangily
34 Comment of complete contentment
37 ___ A. Bank (men's clothier since 1905)
38 Man's name that means "the king"
39 Last word in many company names
40 Tidbit for an echidna
41 Tone-___
42 Of very poor quality, in modern slang
43 Old Model M's and Model T-6s
45 Blues group?: Abbr.
46 It's truly inspired
47 Offerings from Friskies
50 Gradually cut off (from)
54 1962 John Wayne film
55 Hit list
57 Handle, of a sort
58 Descended upon, as mosquitoes might
59 "Another Bud, bud!"
60 Comic con, e.g.

DOWN

1 Prime directive?
2 Nebula Award winner Frederik
3 Guy's gal
4 Pioneering thrash metal band with its own music festival, Gigantour
5 Dating letters
6 Commence-ment
7 Class in which kids may learn about sin?
8 Best-selling game with a hexagonal board
9 College area of study with no application required?
10 On the double
11 Contents of a bowl or a pot
12 Complained loudly and publicly
13 Kir and Campari, for two
14 Stark family member on "Game of Thrones"
21 What the U.S. and Canadian dollars had, roughly, in the early 2010s
23 Made looser or tighter, in a way
26 Opulence
27 Is perfect, clothing-wise
29 It's got its ups and downs
31 Mobile home?
32 Capital on the Balkan Peninsula
34 Barely open
35 It's going downhill
36 Not a team player
42 Often-reddish quartz
44 1990s' ___ Report
48 Crop
49 Something brought to a supermarket

by Sam Trabucco

ACROSS

1 Tarot card, with "the"
5 Bird named for its black-and-white markings
15 Eccentric fashion designer in "The Incredibles"
16 Its deep blue variety is called maxixe
17 Trixie's mom, in the comics
18 Cocktail made from peach schnapps and orange juice
19 Track event
20 Brand once marketed as "The Reincarnation of Tea"
21 Gate announcement, briefly
22 Demand
24 Kind of type
28 Island attire
29 One maturing quickly, informally
30 Skewed
31 Erasable mark
35 Target of some therapy
36 Wrestler Flair
37 It comes from Mars
38 Your heart may go out to it
41 Title for Macbeth
42 Rock and roll, e.g.
43 Their players are often benched
44 Half of an old comedy duo
45 Taboo word
46 Ivy League nickname
48 One of the Everly Brothers
50 Either of the two highest trump cards in euchre
52 Was charming?
56 Queens stadium eponym
57 Body of water between two locks of the Erie Canal
58 The Big Bad Wolf, in old cartoons
59 Reason for going out a lot?
60 Fervor

DOWN

1 Pool surface
2 Sole supporter?
3 Item sold at Burger King but not at most McDonald's
4 Person tasked with locking up
5 Full-figured
6 Peer
7 Hype
8 University of Arkansas mascot
9 One of the March sisters
10 Cooler
11 Portfolio part, for short
12 "Around the World in 80 Days" star, 1956
13 Tech news source
14 Not free to go
23 Pismire
25 Rembrandt or Vermeer
26 "The fierce urgency of now" speaker, familiarly
27 So on and so forth
28 Starch-producing palm tree
29 Oreo ___
31 Small fruit high in pectin
32 "Lemme look!"
33 1939 film banned in the Soviet Union
34 Participants in some awkward meetings
39 Exhibition-funding grp.
40 "Man, it's cold!"
41 Quaint contraction
43 Part of a Rube Goldberg device
44 Dough nut?
45 Uses shamelessly
46 M.B.A. prereq.
47 Singer ___ Del Rey
49 Crate

by Trenton Charlson

51 Balance beam?

53 Poker game tell, perhaps

54 Foofaraw

55 ___ soda

ACROSS

1 Spring report
6 Bad fall
12 Performance bonus
14 Print alternative
15 Place for driving lessons
16 Salves
17 Manner of speaking in eastern Virginia
19 Men
20 Hundred Acre Wood youngster
21 45th anniversary gifts
22 Dangerous toy
24 Charged
25 ___ de boeuf en croûte
26 Brings on
27 Roman god invoked by Iago
28 Leveled
29 Canal sight
30 Tragedy that was first performed in 431 B.C.
31 Don
35 Inits. in a bowling alley
36 Bygone magazine spinoff
37 Linguistic borrowing, as "earworm" from "Ohrwurm"
40 One who gets lots of tweets?
41 World capital on the Rideau Canal
42 Moolah
43 Lead-in to weight
44 Simpson who infamously lip-synched a song on "S.N.L."
45 High and thin, as a voice

DOWN

1 Siamese fighting fish
2 Iroquois Confederacy nation
3 Became impassable, in a way
4 Medal with the dates MDCCCXXXIII–MDCCCXCVI
5 What a business might shift resources to
6 Dances taught by a kumu
7 George Orwell's real first name
8 "Just ___"
9 Branches
10 End up as a wash
11 Surmount
13 Checked out
14 Body in our solar system that was considered a planet in the first half of the 19th century
16 Found a new tenant for
18 Gogol's "___ Bulba"
22 Certain obsessive-compulsive
23 Shiny blowfly
25 Maker of rows
26 Trusted
27 Believers who practice ahimsa, strict nonviolence to all living creatures
28 Strips
29 George ___, co-star with Bette Davis in 11 films, including "Dark Victory" and "Jezebel"
30 Unesco's ___ Fund for Girls' Right to Education
31 Cut off
32 Codeine, for one
33 Went from adagio to largo, say
34 In base 6

by Byron Walden

36 Fleeting moment

38 N.B.A. starter?: Abbr.

39 Reliable

97 ★ ★ ★

ACROSS

1 General plan?
7 Reproductive part
13 Locks that might not be totally secure?
15 Cause of wheezing
16 Put on the line, perhaps
18 Check names
19 It gets cleared for takeoff
21 Bit of gymnastics equipment
22 Important thing to know, if you will
24 Big biceps, in slang
25 Photos from drones, e.g.
26 Trail mix morsel
27 "How ___ it?"
28 Some works by poets laureate
29 Crime for which Al Capone went to prison
33 Yank
34 Put on the line
35 PC "brain"
36 Character raised in "Rosemary's Baby"
38 In the thick of
39 One relatively close either way?
40 Female role in "Pulp Fiction"
41 Silly
42 Pitfall
44 Theater ticket option
46 Debtor's letters
47 Ones flying in circles
48 BBQ offering
50 Settlers of disputes
54 Noted library opened in 2001
55 Traveler who picks up three companions in a classic film
56 Pledge to
57 Ill will

DOWN

1 One-time connection
2 Affected response to an allegation
3 Prickly husk
4 Keeps current
5 First podcast to win a Peabody Award (2015)
6 Job requiring a car, say
7 Fruit in the custard apple family
8 "Here's my two cents . . ."
9 Dump
10 Tony winner set in River City, Iowa
11 "Um . . . er . . ."
12 Doesn't die
14 Singer with the #1 albums "Stars Dance" (2013) and "Revival" (2015)
17 Pie that comes "fully loaded"
20 Green protector
22 Become, finally
23 Colorado's official state dinosaur
24 Wonderful time
25 Tiny bit
27 Roll of bread
29 Road goo
30 Peace sign
31 Pontificate
32 Titian's "Venus Anadyomene," e.g.
34 Lbs. and ozs.
37 Tiny bit
38 "Friends" co-star
41 One of the Gandhis
42 Shankbone
43 Romps
44 Modern handbag portmanteau
45 Shady area
47 Zymurgist's interest

by Andrew J. Ries

49 Animal that doesn't have a sound coming out of its head?

51 Series end

52 P

53 Aleppo's land: Abbr.

98

★★★

ACROSS

1 Calgary nickname, along with "Stampede City"
8 Competitor of Twinings
14 Collapsible chapeau
16 Where Sevastopol is
17 Like Denver
18 Book page size
19 Eat lots of protein and carbs, say
20 Some legal speeders, briefly
22 Cab alternative
23 Pioneering football coach ___ Alonzo Stagg
24 Occupy, as a desk
26 "Let's ___!"
27 "I expected better"
28 They may go on long walks
29 Member of Dubya's cabinet
30 It's filled with energy
32 The Netherlands was the first country to legalize it
35 Celebrated the birth of a child, perhaps
36 Winegrowing region of SW France
37 Them, to us
38 Prefix with tourism or politics
41 "Hmm . . ."
42 Bygone potentates
43 Word with bank or blind
44 Love, by another name
45 Like the ocean
46 Mess up
48 Permanent-press
50 Pogo and others
52 Totally dominating
53 Bad record?
54 Alternatives to S.U.V.s, informally
55 Common "explanation" from a parent

DOWN

1 Private practice?
2 Poppy products
3 "Sure, I guess . . ."
4 Long hauls
5 Island with a state capital
6 Jerked in two directions at once
7 Poke with a lot of needles?
8 Michael ___, "The Office" manager
9 Parentheses, essentially
10 Sloshed
11 Endangered watershed
12 Marine
13 Web-based recovery program, informally
15 Film featuring an assassin from 2029
21 Rubber
25 To a fault
26 Indian flatbreads
28 Trig function
29 Deal in
30 Souchong alternative
31 Boarding points at amusement parks
32 Vessel in a famous 1960s shipwreck
33 Midwest university city
34 Part-time job for many an actor or actress
38 Came after
39 Hannity's former Fox News foil
40 Must pay
42 Sharp tastes
43 Bento box fare
45 Skier Lindsey with three Olympic medals
47 Peak in Thessaly

by Ryan McCarty

49 Bravo, e.g.

51 ___ gow (gambling game played with dominoes)

99 ★★★

ACROSS

1 Wall light
7 "Well, excu-u-use me!"
14 Frisk
15 What short sleeves leave
16 Feebleness
17 Wholly
18 The religiously unaffiliated
19 Wipe out
20 Carrier to Tokyo
21 Monk's title
22 Single-___
24 Twerp
25 Terse response accepting responsibility
27 Unnerving look
30 4K
32 Midwest tribe
33 Private R&R
34 Frustrating place to be stranded
38 Gambling card game that up to 10 may comfortably play at once
40 Involve, as in controversy
41 Some social media celebrities
45 Days of old
46 Decays
47 Pair
49 Org. that penalizes carrying
50 Places where people wear masks, for short
51 Actress Katherine of "27 Dresses"
53 Fool
55 Like well-connected investigative reporters, say
57 Detests
58 "If . . . then" sort of thinker
59 Faux brother of a popular rock group
60 Do a school visit, in a way?
61 Play favorites with

DOWN

1 Rare-earth element named after where it was discovered
2 Engage in some P.D.A.
3 Handy item in the kitchen?
4 The ___ Nugget (alliteratively named newspaper since 1897)
5 English potato chip
6 Subj. of a "Delayed" sign
7 Cheese sometimes flavored with dill
8 Subjects of tests for purity
9 "___ sorry . . ."
10 Beam
11 Illinois college town
12 Key of Mozart's "Requiem"
13 Demesne
15 Greek city visited by Paul before Athens
19 Sized up
23 Stick
24 Like a cloudless night
26 Gets carried away
28 Capturer of an unguarded remark
29 Stick in a cabinet, say
31 Latin 101 word
35 Clear choice for auto buyers
36 Like the 101st Division
37 Skin care product
39 Kind of velocity in planetary physics
40 And others: Abbr.
41 Some social media commenters
42 Kept going and going

by John Guzzetta

43 "We've got the green light"
44 Most common noble gas
48 Hinder
51 "Shoot!"
52 Emmy winner Falco
54 "Heavens to Betsy!"
56 Wine aperitif
57 One of the first artists to incorporate random chance

100 ★★★

ACROSS

1 What takes motion out of motion pictures?
10 Goddess of spring and rebirth
14 Superiority-asserting action
15 Drunk, in modern slang
16 Is to come
17 Wiped out
18 Fair game
19 Parody
21 Certain online food critic
22 Prefix with car
23 Place for a tab
24 Wine lover's favorite team?
26 Persuaded to take a higher-priced option
29 Enemies, in slang
33 Lose balance
34 Women who were legally permitted to drive for the first time in 2018
35 Response to someone with unrealistic hopes
38 "Take your time"
39 Word whose musical sense was added to Merriam-Webster dictionaries in 1986
40 Competitor of Petro-Canada
41 Green-light
42 Some baskets
44 Business card abbr.
45 California W.N.B.A. team, on scoreboards
47 "This party's poppin'!"
52 Boo-boos
55 Off guard
56 Discover serendipitously
57 Article of summer wear
59 ___ Montoya, swordsman in "The Princess Bride"
60 Woman's name that's an anagram of INTERNEES
61 Body parts that sound like some units of measure
62 Start of an anti-coal petition

DOWN

1 Spread out
2 Fabric whose name is French for "cloth"
3 Tom ___, co-star of Marilyn Monroe in "The Seven Year Itch"
4 "Venus and the Cat" author
5 Storage site
6 "Let me assist you"
7 Like some rec leagues
8 Palindromic woman's name
9 Cry on a battlefield
10 Unlikely entrant in a Westminster show
11 Some demographic data
12 Emphasized
13 Deals with
15 Mai ___
20 Arrow on a screen
22 Field for gamers
25 Kind of project for a hardware store customer, in brief
27 Goddess of peace
28 Person whom people take their complaints to, informally
29 It can pass when you pass
30 Connection to the outside world
31 Spongelike
32 Proof of purchase, perhaps
36 Certain connection for a 30-Down, for short
37 Negotiating partner with G.M.
43 Natural ager
46 Flicked, in a way
48 Competitor of Stearns & Foster
49 Music store category
50 Words before know, care or mind
51 Most serious kind of flu
53 Fad game of the 1990s
54 Unnamed individual from Italy

by Anna Gundlach and Erik Agard

55 It reaches to touch one's hand

58 What you can take that I can't?

SMART PUZZLES

Presented with Style

Available at your local bookstore or online at
us.macmillan.com/series/thenewyorktimescrosswordpuzzles

ST. MARTIN'S GRIFFIN

ANSWERS

1

S	C	A	M	S		D	A	M	E		A	F	T	S
O	H	F	U	N		R	I	A	L		C	L	A	P
X	A	C	T	O		E	M	M	A	S	T	O	N	E
	L	E	E	R	S		A	B	I	T		O	L	E
Q	U	A	R	T	E	R	T	O	N	E		R	I	D
V	P	S		S	T	E		E	L	N	I	N	O	
C	A	T	O		A	T	M	S		M	A	T	E	S
		M	E	T	R	I	C	T	O	N				
O	C	T	A	D		O	D	O	R		A	S	E	A
B	L	O	N	D	E		R	I	G		P	R	Y	
L	A	S		I	M	E	A	N	C	O	M	E	O	N
A	P	T		E	A	R	N		E	P	I	C	S	
S	T	A	N	D	I	N	G	O		A	N	T	I	C
T	O	D	O		L	I	L	A		S	C	R	O	D
S	N	A	G		S	E	E	K		T	E	E	N	S

2

T	W	O		R	E	I	G	N	S		S	L	O	G
A	I	R		O	C	T	A	N	E		T	A	K	E
C	P	A		W	H	E	R	E	S	O	E	V	E	R
T	E	N	S	I	O	N	S		A	B	R	A	D	E
		G	E	N			C	M	O	N				
A	V	E	N	G	E	R		R	E	L		U	V	W
M	A	R	S		G	A	Z	A		I	N	N	E	R
E	L	I	E		O	P	E	D	S		O	P	R	Y
M	I	N	D	Y		I	D	L	E		R	A	G	E
O	D	D		A	C	E		E	M	P	T	I	E	R
		C	H	A	R			L	O	D				
S	O	S	O	O	N		I	S	T	A	N	B	U	L
P	R	E	M	O	N	I	T	I	O	N		I	T	O
E	Z	R	A		E	M	E	R	G	E		L	E	A
C	O	B	S		S	P	R	E	A	D		L	S	D

3

G	O	S	S	I	P		T	G	I		M	E	S	S
L	A	M	A	R	R		R	E	D	D	I	W	I	P
E	T	A	L	I	I		A	L	I	E	N	A	T	E
N	H	L		S	N	O	W			A	G	N	E	W
	S	L	Y		T	E	L	L	A	L	L			
	W	E	B	M	D		A	T	T	E	M	P	T	
S	H	O	P	P	E		T	I	L		R	U	L	E
T	A	R		A	D	M	I	R	A	L		M	I	A
E	L	L	S		I	O	N		R	O	B	B	E	R
M	O	D	E	L	U	N		I	G	L	O	O		
	V	A	M	O	O	S	E		P	J	S			
E	S	S	E	S			P	A	R	K		U	P	C
D	O	W	N	S	I	Z	E		A	N	E	M	I	A
N	A	U	T	I	C	A	L		C	O	M	B	E	D
A	R	M	Y		U	P	S		E	X	T	O	L	S

4

5

6

7

S	A	W	I	I	■	E	C	H	O	■	V	A	N	S
P	L	A	N	T	■	D	A	M	P	■	O	B	I	E
E	L	V	I	S	A	N	D	M	E	■	R	U	L	E
W	I	E	■	O	J	A	Y	■	R	I	T	T	E	R
S	E	D	A	K	A	■	■	M	A	C	E	■	■	
■	■	O	A	X	A	C	A	M	E	X	I	C	O	
S	P	I	N	Y	■	D	R	Y	A	D	■	T	A	Z
P	A	N	E	■	D	E	I	O	N	■	G	E	T	Z
U	P	N	■	W	A	X	E	R	■	C	O	N	E	Y
D	I	S	C	O	V	E	R	S	I	O	N	■	■	
■	■	E	R	I	C	■	T	O	G	A	E	D		
U	N	J	A	M	S	■	B	A	C	K	■	U	V	A
C	O	O	S	■	C	A	R	D	H	O	L	D	E	R
L	I	N	E	■	U	T	A	H	■	F	A	I	N	T
A	R	I	D	■	P	E	N	D	■	F	O	O	T	S

8

S	P	A	M	■	M	E	A	L	S	■	H	O	L	A
T	E	R	I	■	A	B	B	O	T	■	A	R	O	D
A	S	O	F	■	I	B	E	L	I	E	V	E	S	O
N	O	N	F	A	T	■	A	R	R	E	S	T	S	
■	■	S	N	A	R	F	■	S	I	A	■	■		
O	R	G	■	N	I	E	L	S	■	C	H	A	S	M
P	E	R	S	E	■	B	A	T	C	H	E	D	I	T
E	R	A	T	■	B	O	X	E	D	■	A	S	T	O
R	O	M	E	■	R	O	S	E	S	■	R	A	P	S
A	L	M	A	M	A	T	E	R	■	A	T	L	A	S
S	L	Y	L	Y	■	S	E	E	M	S	■	E	T	A
■	■	A	B	C	■	D	R	U	I	D	■	■		
A	R	I	K	A	R	A	■	R	A	R	I	N	G	
G	O	S	I	D	E	W	A	Y	S	■	U	S	E	R
A	R	E	S	■	T	E	H	E	E	■	M	O	R	E
R	Y	E	S	■	E	D	I	T	S	■	S	N	O	W

9

H	E	M	S	■	E	L	M	O	■	B	A	L	D	S
A	V	E	C	■	M	E	A	L	■	C	L	A	R	K
L	I	F	E	G	U	A	R	D	■	C	A	S	E	Y
F	L	I	N	T	■	P	L	E	A	■	■	C	A	L
W	E	R	E	O	N	■	A	N	D	S	O	A	M	I
A	Y	S	■	S	E	A	■	■	S	A	D	L	O	T
Y	E	T	I	■	L	I	E	S	■	L	O	A	N	■
■	■	F	I	L	M	L	O	V	E	R	■	■		
■	S	H	O	D	■	S	I	R	I	■	S	H	E	L
G	O	A	L	I	E	■	T	E	M	■	O	V	A	
H	A	N	D	G	R	I	P	■	W	E	S	L	E	Y
O	K	S	■	A	M	O	S	■	R	H	I	N	E	
U	S	O	F	A	■	P	O	L	I	C	E	D	O	G
L	U	L	U	S	■	E	L	A	N	■	B	A	N	G
S	P	O	R	K	■	I	S	M	S	■	A	Y	E	S

10

```
B O L T █ B L O C █ A B A S E
I T O O █ L A L A █ C A M U S
D O U G █ U T A H █ T R O M P
█ H I G H D E F I N I T I O N
█ S L O G █ █ L I V E █
█ O V E R E X P L A I N E D
A N I █ N O V A █ █ A D D O N
H E L P █ N I N T H █ S N U B
H A L L S █ D A U B █ A S A
█ M E A N I N G O F L I F E
█ T O D O █ █ F A C E █
L E X I C O G R A P H E R S
A R E N A █ G O G O █ A B O Y
G I N U P █ I D E S █ G E N E
S C A M S █ N E S T █ E R G S
```

11

```
C H A S E █ S T O R M █ A P P
A E S O P █ I O N I A █ W A R
S I T T I N G D U C K █ K E A
E R A █ S E N D S █ E L W A Y
█ █ S O H O █ A S I A N S
S T A N D I N G O R D E R █
A E R I E S █ R I C O █ D A B
A A R P █ A O L █ T A M E
B R O █ A U R A █ S P I G O T
█ W A L K I N G P A P E R S
I N H A L E █ E A R S █
G E E S E █ S O N I A █ P A W
L E A █ R U N N I N G J O K E
O D D █ G R A C E █ O L L I E
O S S █ Y I P E S █ N O E N D
```

12

```
I M O F F █ S P U R N █ P U G
S O L A R █ T A G U P █ I P O
A L L T O G E T H E R █ A F T
Y E A █ S T A T █ S N O B
█ A T O M I C T H E O R Y █
A L W A Y S █ R E A C T █
M O O R █ A S I A M █ U M A
A I R P O R T T E R M I N A L
S N L █ S E E P S █ N E I L
█ D A L A I █ F A I R L Y
A N C H O R T E N A N T █
C O L A █ B O N D █ M V P
U S A █ T H E E I G H T I E S
T I S █ S E A R S █ O A T E S
E R S █ K N U T E █ W R E S T
```

13

I	D	T	A	G			A	B	S			R	A	S	T	A
F	O	R	C	E			M	E	W			E	A	T	O	N
F	R	E	E	T	R	A	D	E			F	R	O	N	T	
Y	A	K			B	O	S	S	E	S			P	O	S	H
			B	U	D	S			T	H	E			D	I	E
C	H	E	E	S	E			D	E	A	D	C	A	L	M	
C	O	M	F	Y			T	O	N	G	U	E	S			
S	O	B	E			N	A	M	E	S			L	I	F	E
		A	L	R	O	K	E	R			S	E	D	A	N	
B	U	R	L	I	V	E	S			S	P	R	E	A	D	
I	N	K			G	A	S			P	L	A	Y			
A	W	E	D			S	A	V	I	O	R			L	E	O
N	O	D	U	H			B	I	L	G	E	P	U	M	P	
C	R	O	N	E			O	N	E			M	E	R	I	T
A	N	N	E	X			W	E	D			E	W	E	R	S

14

M	E	T	A	D	A	T	A			D	E	F	A	N	G
O	X	Y	M	O	R	O	N			I	L	L	S	E	E
S	H	R	I	N	K	I	N	G	V	I	O	L	E	T	
H	O	E	D					A	R	E	S	O			
E	R	S			E	N	G	L	I	S	H	R	O	S	E
S	T	E	L	L	A	R			P	T	A			O	L	D
			A	L	I	A	S					S	N	U	G
F	L	O	W	E	R	Y	L	A	N	G	U	A	G	E	
L	O	P	S					O	C	E	A	N			
A	K	A			A	T	M			T	A	R	G	E	T	S
G	I	L	D	T	H	E	L	I	L	Y			L	E	A
			O	B	E	S	E					G	N	A	T
A	S	F	R	E	S	H	A	S	A	D	A	I	S	Y	
W	O	E	I	S	I			D	O	G	O	W	N	E	R
E	L	E	C	T	S			S	T	E	W	P	O	T	S

15

S	P	E	W			P	I	T	S			B	O	S	S	Y
L	A	V	A			O	P	E	N			I	R	A	T	E
A	C	I	D			T	R	E	E			F	A	U	L	T
T	E	L	E	P	H	O	N	E	P	O	L	E			
			D	O	O	M			Z	A	C			R	A	T
N	E	G			S	L	I	D	E	T	A	C	K	L	E
E	X	A	M			E	S	O			L	O	R	A	X
A	C	N	E			S	E	N	D	S			E	A	S	T
R	E	D	D	I				O	I	L			D	U	K	E
B	L	O	O	P	E	R	R	E	E	L			T	A	D
Y	S	L			A	G	E			T	E	E	S			
			F	I	D	G	E	T	S	P	I	N	N	E	R
C	H	I	R	P			D	U	O	S			I	O	N	A
T	E	N	O	R			E	N	D	O			F	R	O	S
R	H	I	N	O			D	E	A	N			F	I	S	H

16

S	H	O	O		S	O	F	I	A		J	A	D	A
K	E	R	R		A	W	A	S	H		E	X	I	T
I	M	A	C		W	I	T	H	C	H	E	E	S	E
M	E	T	H	A	N	E			H	O	P			
S	N	E	E	R			S	C	O	T	S	M	E	N
	S	E	E	B	E	L	O	W		O	M	G		
	E	M	T		T	A	T	A		A	M	O	C	O
	C	A	R	B	O	N	D	I	O	X	I	D	E	
M	O	L	A	R		I	A	M	B		L	Y	E	
A	N	A		E	A	S	T	S	I	D	E			
J	O	R	D	A	C	H	E		I	P	A	D	S	
	O	T	C		A	M	M	O	N	I	A			
J	O	H	N	H	U	G	H	E	S		S	T	A	T
U	H	U	H		S	T	A	R	R		T	I	N	A
G	O	G	O		E	S	T	O	P		S	C	A	N

17

A	G	E	G	A	P		D	R	I	P		S	N	O
P	I	N	A	T	A		R	E	B	A		E	O	N
U	N	C	L	I	P		J	E	O	P	A	R	D	Y
		A	L	E	S		S	O	A	P	B	O	X	
A	L	E	X	T	R	E	B	E	K		T	I	N	E
F	U	R	Y		M	R	I	S		M	E	A	T	S
E	S	L		C	O	I	N		G	A	S			
W	H	E	E	L	O	F		F	O	R	T	U	N	E
		F	A	N		F	A	D	E		G	E	D	
S	T	R	I	P		Q	U	I	P		S	L	A	G
A	R	A	L		V	A	N	N	A	W	H	I	T	E
W	E	G	E	T	I	T		T	R	I	O			
P	A	T	S	A	J	A	K		E	S	P	I	E	S
I	T	O		L	A	R	A		N	E	P	A	L	I
T	S	P		L	Y	I	N		T	R	E	M	O	R

18

U	S	E	D		O	M	A	N	I		A	C	T	S
N	U	D	E		R	A	T	O	N		B	A	R	E
C	B	G	B		E	A	T	A	T		S	L	A	W
A	W	E		M	C	M	A	H	O	N		V	I	A
S	A	I	D	O	K			W	A	K	I	N	G	
T	Y	N	A	N		A	M	S		S	E	N	S	E
	M	A	M	M	A	L	I	A	N					
M	O	V	E		B	Y	N	E	S		O	V	E	R
A	P	E		A	P	S	E	S		A	V	A		
N	E	R	V	E		O	P	P		H	O	M	E	R
U	N	T	I	L		E	R	A		A	D	O	R	E
	B	E	E	B		H	E	P		Z	O	O	M	
M	A	X	W	E	L	L	A	N	D	E	R	S	O	N
A	R	E		R	O	E	D	E	E	R		E	R	E
A	S	S		T	A	R	S	A	L	S		D	E	W

19

```
L A P D  ▪  ▪ A F L A C ▪ S W A B ▪
A R E A S ▪ M I A M I ▪ ▪ M I C E ▪
D R A M A T I S P E R S O N A E
E A R ▪ H I G H ▪ ▪ C O R G I S ▪
S U L T A N O F B R U N E I ▪
▪ ▪ I R T ▪ R O O S ▪ ▪ S N U B
S U N D A E ▪ Y A W ▪ ▪ G R O
T H E E N D ▪ ▪ I S N I G H
A N A ▪ ▪ D O H ▪ N E A T E R
G O R P ▪ S O B A ▪ L X I ▪
▪ F I G H T I N G I L L I N I
A S A S E T ▪ G E N E ▪ X E R
B A T T L E O F T H E S I N A I
L M A O ▪ T R U E R ▪ S O A R S
Y E L L ▪ L E N N Y ▪ ▪ N Y S E
```

20

```
D A R N S ▪ I S M S ▪ L A S S
O R I O N ▪ S T E P ▪ O W E N
B I G C O M P A N Y ▪ V E G A
B O O H O O ▪ G U I D E D O G
S T R E T C H ▪ N U S ▪
▪ H A I R G R E A S E
N A M ▪ B A S T E ▪ E A R E D
S C A L A ▪ F I G ▪ S T O L E
F A R A D ▪ U S E R S ▪ D A N
W I C K E D N I N E ▪
▪ E G O ▪ T A G A L O G
M A K E G O O D ▪ D E F U S E
U B E R ▪ F R O Z E N O N C E
S I R I ▪ U S N A ▪ T O G A S
E T R E ▪ S O A P ▪ S T E R E
```

21

```
C A B O ▪ G A B ▪ L A B R A T
A L E S ▪ E R A ▪ E N O U G H
P A T R I L E Y ▪ N A T G E O
▪ A I M ▪ S O N G ▪ T E N T
P E T C A T ▪ N E T W O R T H
O N E ▪ C U R E D H A M ▪
M D S ▪ G E T ▪ F U J I
P I T B O S S ▪ N I T P I C K
▪ T S A R ▪ A I R ▪ M A I
▪ T E E N B E A T ▪ M R T
P O T H O L E S ▪ N O T Y E T
O V E R ▪ S E E M ▪ M U D ▪
P U T O U T ▪ N U T B R E A D
E L R O P O ▪ C S I ▪ B A B Y
S E A M A N ▪ E S P ▪ O N C E
```

22

E	G	G	S	■	B	O	B	C	A	T	■	A	R	C
B	A	R	E	■	C	L	A	I	R	E	■	D	E	O
B	L	A	N	K	C	A	N	V	A	S	■	L	T	D
■	Y	A	O	■	■	D	I	R	T	■	I	R	E	
K	E	A	T	O	N	■	B	L	A	C	K	B	O	X
A	L	R	O	K	E	R	■	■	T	A	O			
P	I	E	R	■	N	E	A	T	■	S	I	R	E	S
U	S	A	■	T	A	N	L	I	N	E	■	E	N	O
T	A	S	T	E	■	T	A	D	A	■	E	D	N	A
■	■	A	A	A	■	E	V	E	N	S	U	P		
G	O	L	D	R	I	N	G	■	I	R	A	Q	I	S
A	P	E	■	T	R	E	O	■	I	C	U			
D	I	M	■	A	B	S	T	R	A	C	T	A	R	T
O	N	O	■	P	U	T	T	E	D	■	E	R	O	S
T	E	N	■	E	S	S	A	Y	S	■	D	E	E	P

23

T	A	P	E	R	■	P	A	P	A	■	A	B	C	S
I	L	L	B	E	■	E	D	E	N	■	S	L	O	T
D	O	U	B	L	E	C	H	I	N	■	S	I	N	E
Y	E	S	■	O	R	T	O	■	K	I	N	D	A	
■	■	M	A	G	I	C	K	I	N	G	D	O	M	
T	R	E	A	D	O	N	■	N	O	E	N	D		
R	O	M	P	■	■	S	E	T	A	■	A	R	M	
A	M	P	■	J	U	G	H	E	A	D	■	T	O	E
P	A	L	■	E	L	L	E	■	■	E	E	L	S	
■	O	R	F	E	O	■	G	U	E	S	S	E	S	
S	A	Y	A	F	E	W	W	O	R	D	S			
T	U	M	M	Y	■	A	U	D	I	■	W	O	O	
A	R	E	A	■	D	I	S	G	U	S	T	I	N	G
L	A	N	D	■	A	C	N	E	■	O	W	N	E	R
E	S	T	A	■	B	E	T	S	■	N	O	O	S	E

24

C	R	U	S	H	■	B	A	S	E	■	M	O	H	S
H	E	N	I	E	■	O	X	E	N	■	I	R	A	N
I	T	S	M	Y	T	R	E	A	T	■	C	I	T	I
C	A	N	I	S	E	E	■	■	T	R	E	E	D	
O	P	A	L	■	D	R	I	N	K	S	O	N	M	E
S	E	G	A	L	■	S	N	E	A	K	■	T	A	S
■	■	R	O	N	■	S	T	L	■	W	A	I	T	
I	L	L	G	E	T	T	H	E	B	I	L	L		
A	T	O	Y	■	W	R	Y	■	L	I	Z			
N	C	C	■	I	D	O	L	S	■	C	A	S	C	A
Y	O	U	R	M	O	N	E	Y	S	■	R	A	H	S
L	U	T	E	S	■	■	N	O	O	D	G	E	S	
U	P	I	N	■	N	O	G	O	O	D	H	E	R	E
C	L	O	D	■	G	R	A	D	■	D	A	L	I	S
K	E	N	S	■	O	O	P	S	■	S	T	Y	E	S

25

```
P A S H A . . O S L O . S O N
F R E E D . C A R O M . U Z I
F I T F O R A K I N G . P A X
T A O . A B E L . . M E R E
. N A T I O N A L P A R K S
S C H M I D T . N E A R .
H E A P S . S K E T C H U P
U R L . T R E A D . I N O
T A L K S H O W . L O T U S
. I C E D . A B O U T M E
T H E W H O L E T R U T H .
H E M I . A M O R . E C O
E L M . C I V I L R I G H T S
F L Y . O D E L L . T I A R A
T A S . D O R Y . S L Y L Y
```

26

```
M L K J R . T S K S . V A T S
E I E I O . O H I O . I D I E
W I N G S P R E A D . E V E R
. S C A R E S . T W I B E
C Y D . O W E N . N I S S A N
R E U B E N . D I D . E R E
Y O R E . S T P E T E
W A T C H Y O U R S T E P
. H O P E S O . A L O U
G A B . I P O . C A R E O F
A D R E P S . F I A T . A F C
W H A M S . N I M R O D
K E P I . L A N D S L I D E S
E R A T . E S A U . L E E R S
R E D S . D A L E . S T E R N
```

27

```
A N K L E . N I C H E . D A S
T A N Y A . U S H E R . O C T
F R E E C Y C L I N G . E T A
I R E . H U L A . S O P S U P
R A B E . K E N T . A N A L
S T O P . S I D E H U S T L E
T O N I C . S E E S T
. R E L O A D . S H A L O M
. E A S E S . F I L A S
D R O P T H E M I C . F I N E
E O N S . P I N E . E V A N
N O T Y E T . R E N D . E G O
T M I . K I C K S T A R T E R
A I M . E L I A S . T E T R A
L E E . S T A T E . A M I S S
```

28

D	Q	E	D		M	A	C	R	O		O	D	D	S
O	U	Z	O		A	D	L	E	R		R	E	E	L
L	I	P	S	E	R	V	I	C	E		A	G	E	E
A	N	A		S	L	I	M			B	L	A	R	E
P	O	S		C	O	L	B	E	R	T	B	U	M	P
S	A	S	H	A				R	O	W		L	E	O
		O	P	E	R	A	N	T		A	L	A	N	
	T	E	L	E	V	I	S	I	O	N	S	E	T	
H	A	N	D		I	N	H	E	R	I	T			
I	T	S		B	A	G			C	O	U	P	E	
G	O	L	D	E	N	S	P	I	K	E		M	A	X
H	O	A	R	D		A	N	E	T		L	E	I	
L	I	V	E		V	O	L	L	E	Y	B	A	L	L
O	N	E	G		I	D	E	A	L		Y	U	L	E
W	E	D	S		M	E	O	W	S		E	T	A	S

29

P	A	I	R		S	I	L	O	S		W	A	S	P
U	L	N	A		K	N	A	V	E		A	U	T	O
T	I	N	F	O	I	L	H	A	T		T	R	O	D
		A	T	B	A	T			R	E	I	N	S	
S	O	P		O	U	T	I	N	F	O	R	C	E	
W	R	I	T	E	M	E		E	A	S	Y			
A	N	N	A			I	R	I	S		A	G	O	
Y	O	U	R	E	I	N	F	O	R	I	T	N	O	W
S	T	P		A	C	E	S			H	I	D	E	
		S	T	A	R		S	P	I	E	S	O	N	
	B	R	A	I	N	F	O	O	D	S		E	T	S
P	L	A	I	N			A	V	I	L	A			
R	I	N	D		I	N	S	I	D	E	I	N	F	O
I	N	K	S		T	R	I	E	D		M	I	L	D
M	I	S	O		T	A	S	T	Y		S	P	U	D

30

H	A	M	M	Y			S	P	F		L	U	B	E
A	P	B	I	O		C	H	E	R		A	P	O	P
R	E	A	D	Y	W	H	E	N	Y	O	U	A	R	E
			J	O	N	I			B	U	N	G	E	E
	L	I	U		B	L	U		R	I	C	A		
D	A	N	N	Y	A	I	N	G	E		H	I	S	S
A	T	S	E	A		S	E	A	M		N	I	T	
M	I	T		P	R	E	C	E	D	E		S	M	U
U	N	I		S	O	A	R		S	I	T	O	N	
P	A	N	S		B	R	E	A	T	H	M	I	N	T
		C	H	A	I		W	W	I		A	T	E	
O	B	T	A	I	N			A	L	E	C			
S	O	U	N	D	S	L	I	K	E	A	P	L	A	N
L	O	A	D		O	G	R	E		C	R	E	M	E
O	N	L	Y		N	A	E			H	O	I	S	T

31

S	H	U	T	S		N	A	S	A	L			B	Y	O	B
H	A	D	A	T		O	V	I	N	E		I	O	W	A	
I	H	O	P	E		T	I	L	D	E		G	R	E	Y	
V	A	N	I	L	L	A	S	K	Y		U	B	E	R	S	
			O	M	I	T			E	T	T	A			
C	H	O	C	O	L	A	T	E	T	H	U	N	D	E	R
L	E	I	A			L	I	N		A	R	G	Y	L	E
I	A	L		C	A	L	M	D	O	W	N		L	A	N
P	R	E	F	A	B		E	E	L		M	A	N	E	
S	T	R	A	W	B	E	R	R	Y	B	L	O	N	D	E
			R	E	A	L			M	O	A	N			
S	O	S	A	D		N	E	A	P	O	L	I	T	A	N
A	V	O	W		M	I	A	M	I		A	K	I	T	A
T	A	D	A		A	N	T	I	C		L	E	D	O	N
S	L	A	Y		P	O	S	E	S		A	R	E	N	A

32

M	O	P	S		C	H	A	I		P	A	S	S	
E	P	I	C		F	O	R	T		R	I	C	E	S
W	A	S	H	R	O	O	M	S		O	G	R	E	S
L	L	A	M	A		T	E	M	P	T		E	I	N
			E	N	D		D	E	B	R	I	E	F	S
N	E	W	A	G	E	R			S	U	N	N	I	
A	C	E	R		J	U	L	Y		D	I	S	C	O
A	H	L		V	A	M	O	O	S	E		H	A	D
N	O	C	H	E		P	O	G	O		T	O	R	O
	L	O	O	N	S		A	R	B	I	T	E	R	
C	O	M	E	D	I	A	N		T	O	M			
I	C	E		E	L	S	E	S		Z	I	P	P	Y
G	A	M	U	T		C	A	N	O	O	D	L	E	S
S	T	A	R	T		A	T	I	T		L	I	T	E
	E	T	N	A		P	O	P	S		Y	E	A	R

33

T	A	R	O	T		A	W	E	D		R	O	P	E
U	N	I	O	N		M	A	T	A		O	B	E	Y
N	I	G	H	T	N	I	G	H	T		A	N	N	E
E	M	U			O	D	E		A	L	M	O	N	D
R	E	P	O	S	T	S		E	S	S	E	X		
		W	H	I	T	E	W	E	D	D	I	N	G	
P	A	S	E	O		P	E	T		O	I	L		
E	L	U	D	E		U	S	S		S	A	U	C	E
R	O	N		C	F	O		I	B	S	E	N		
M	U	S	H	R	O	O	M	B	A	L	L			
	C	O	O	P	S		A	T	T	E	S	T	S	
P	A	R	O	D	Y		S	N	O		T	O	E	
A	G	E	D		C	A	P	A	N	D	G	O	W	N
T	R	E	E		A	L	A	N		N	A	M	E	S
H	A	N	D		T	I	N	A		A	P	P	L	E

34

```
P A L L   . M U F F . . A G E
I D E A S . E S A I . B R A G
S H A R K . M A R G A R I T A
M O N D A L E . T R A D E D .
O C T . . O S C A R I I . . .
. O B I T . R U E . N A I F .
L A T E N T . E K E . L I S A
G R E E K . A A S . B E R E T
B E N E . W C S . M O S S E S
T A T A . E E E . E A S T . .
. . T S A R D O M . . R O E .
C O H E I R . D O G B E R T .
C H E R R Y P I E . P E A C H
T I E S . O H N O . A D M A N
V O L . F I N N . . E S S O .
```

35

```
G R A B B E D . H A S I D I M
L E C A R R E . E X O D E R M
I C E N I N E . A M A L G A M
D E S K T O P [WALL] P A P E R .
E D I T . S N O . E S P . . .
D E T E S T S . P S A L M . .
. L O R A [WALL] A S E P S I S
W O L F O F [WALL] S T R E E T
P I P E T T E . H E A L . . .
U S E R S . E N S U R E S . .
P E N . P I P . N A M E . . .
. S T O N E [WALL] J A C K S O N
L A L A K E R . E N L I S T S
S T O K E R S . S T A N L E E
D E T E N T E . S I N G E R S
```

36

```
. G I F T S . . S W I F T .
M I N I S K I . M I L L I .
W I L D T H I N G . I N K I N
I L L S . I R I S . L I S P S
I D S . I R T . T W I N . . .
. I N T . C R I N G I N G . .
R I F F S . B L I N G . K I R
I S I S . B R I N K . Z I T I
G I N . S L I N G . M I D S T
S T I F L I N G . W I G . . .
. R I N G . S I X . F B I . .
S P R I G . I N I T . S I R S
I R I S H . T I G H T K N I T
T I N C T . C H I M I N G . .
S I K H S . . . S N I P S . .
```

37

```
V E S P A   L E G S   S P O T S
A S K E W   A V O N   A R N I E
N S Y N C   R A T E   N O B E L
C A P T O R I N H A N D   U R L
E Y E   M I A     K A R A T
    B E A T T H E R A P T O R
R A T I O N   W A R Y   P O L O
A L I G N   B I T S   S E N D S
C O M A   E A C H   O C A S E Y
K E E P I T R E A L T O R
    B E N T O   A T F   G I G
T H O   C A N T O R O F C O R N
O O M P H   E A S Y   S O F I A
A B B I E   S C A N   A M E N S
D O S E D   S T Y X   T O R A H
```

38

```
L A S H   A D D S   E T C H
A L I A S   R O U E   S O H O
B U T T W E I G H T   T O A T
T M I   A D A M     B E L T S
E N D I N G   A I S L E B E E
C A L M S E A   S P A   A A A
H E E D   C P L U S   R U T
      B U Y C H A N T S
T H E   S E E I N   H O S T
R O Y   E T S   D O L U N C H
E W E G U I S E   P A N E R A
S T R A P   L I A M   Y E T
T R O Y   C Z E C H P L E A S
L U L L   S I C K   S O A M I
E E L Y   I T T Y   T R O T
```

39

```
J E S T E D   T W E N   P A R
A L P A C A   H A E Y L L E H
M E L L O N   E C N U O E N O
P A I L   S O L O S   L A E M
A N T I H E R O   Y A C S I B
C O R E A   S O S   S A E D I
K R U S T Y   K U E H T
S S N   R E V I V E R   F E D
    L E N I N   R A B O S I
T I D E D   M G M   M A R C S
U N E A S E   G A T S S E O G
S L E D   S E L E S   A S R U
C O M O E S T A   A L L E T S
A V E N G E R S   R E T E E T
N E D   O X E S   S E S N E S
```

40

```
C R A B ■ A R C S ■ H O T E L
L I T E ■ P E R P ■ A W A K E
O V A L ■ S T A R ■ N I X E D
D E L I V E R Y A D D E R ■ ■
S T L E O ■ A O N E ■ ■ E L K
■ ■ F L Y I N G B U T T E R ■
S S S ■ E N S ■ ■ S A U T E ■
C A T N A P S ■ A T E C R O W
A D R E P ■ ■ C N N ■ N N E ■
B L O W U P M A T T E R ■ ■ ■
S Y N ■ H E R E ■ M A G M A ■
■ G E N D E R N E U T R A L ■
L E M M E ■ M A N X ■ T I T O
A W A I T ■ A C A I ■ A M E N
V E N T S ■ W E S T ■ N Y S E
```

41

```
R C A S ■ A I M ■ B A H A I S
E R I ■ C I D L E ■ A R A R A T
V ∞ D ∞ D O L L ■ S C H E M A
S N A P E ■ T I S ■ A T F
■ S E A L ■ F ∞ L P R ∞ F
O D D ■ R E G I N A L ■
C R I T I C A L ■ D E C C A
T ∞ R I C H F O R M Y B L ∞ D
O P E R A ■ M O U S S A K A
■ E N C A S E S ■ D E M
F ∞ T S T ∞ L ■ S T A G
A L I ■ L E T ■ L A N D O
C A M E R A ■ G ∞ G ∞ E Y E S
E L E V E N ■ I N A F L A S H
T A X A C T ■ F A B ■ S H I A
```

42

```
A L I ■ T S T R A P ■ S C O W
C A D ■ A P I A R Y ■ H O N E
R P I ■ G R A P E L E A V E S
O L D F O E S ■ P O N D E R ■
B A N A N A ■ B A N C ■ R O I
A T O M ■ D A I S ■ L E M O N
T A T ■ E O N S ■ T O T E M S
■ F R U I T L E S S ■
A F L O A T ■ R O L E ■ B R A
D R O P S ■ K O O L ■ E R A S
M A V ■ I N E S ■ S P L I T S
■ T E E N I E ■ M A E S T R O
O R A N G E P E E L S ■ C A R
H O L D ■ C A T S I T ■ O C T
O W L S ■ E T C H E S ■ M E S
```

43

C	O	H	E	R	E	N	T	■	E	K	G	■	T	E	A
A	P	O	L	O	G	I	A	■	Z	E	R	O	I	N	G
N	E	W	Y	O	R	K	S	A	R	E	A	C	O	D	E
A	N	I	■	S	E	I	■	P	A	N	I	C	■		
D	E	E	D	■	T	T	O	P	■	L	U	C	A	S	
A	D	M	I	T	■	A	L	L	A	N	■	R	O	S	E
■	A	S	O	F	■	D	E	M	O	S	■	N	I	X	
L	I	N	C	O	L	N	S	B	I	R	T	H	D	A	Y
O	D	D	■	N	I	E	C	E	■	M	E	M	O	■	
K	I	E	V	■	T	E	H	E	E	■	W	O	M	B	S
I	D	L	E	R	■	O	S	I	S	■	S	I	R	E	
■	R	E	C	T	O	■	S	I	S	■	N	A	P		
H	2	O	S	B	O	I	L	I	N	G	P	O	I	N	T
A	1	S	A	U	C	E	■	S	E	M	I	N	U	D	E
W	2	S	■	S	A	D	■	T	R	A	N	S	M	I	T

44

S	U	N	■	F	I	R	E	■	M	O	T	H	E	R
O	R	I	■	U	R	A	L	■	A	D	W	A	R	E
L	I	B	R	E	T	T	O	■	D	E	A	L	I	N
■	B	E	G	■	A	P	A	R	T	■	L	E	D	
H	E	L	L	O	■	T	E	L	E	S	C	O	P	E
O	R	E	■	E	A	S	T	■	R	O	A	R		
L	A	R	G	E	S	T	■	E	C	R	U	■		
A	S	S	O	R	T	■	O	P	E	R	A	S		
■	T	E	E	N	■	E	N	G	L	I	S	H		
C	I	T	Y	■	A	R	S	E	■	N	C	O		
I	N	E	E	D	A	N	A	P	■	N	I	G	H	T
U	S	A	■	I	V	A	N	A	■	O	C	T		
D	I	P	D	Y	E	■	K	N	O	C	K	O	U	T
A	D	O	R	E	R	■	L	O	C	H	■	S	P	A
D	E	T	E	R	S	■	E	L	S	E	■	S	I	X

45

J	E	E	P	■	L	O	T	S	■	P	R	A	M	S
A	C	D	C	■	D	A	W	N	■	R	E	G	A	L
B	O	I	L	■	T	R	I	O	■	O	M	A	N	I
■	T	A	K	E	S	T	W	O	T	O	T	A	N	
Z	O	M	B	I	E	■	S	Y	N	E	■	E	G	G
I	R	E	■	N	T	S	■	M	I	S	S	E	S	
O	D	N	I	G	H	T	I	R	E	N	E	■		
N	O	U	N	■	E	C	U	■	W	I	N	D		
■	C	A	R	M	E	N	S	A	N	D	I	E		
L	F	G	A	M	E	■	T	A	X	■	A	T	E	
E	R	L	■	M	A	S	C	■	T	E	A	R	E	D
G	O	O	V	E	R	T	H	E	E	D	G	E	■	
A	T	B	A	T	■	A	I	D	E	■	E	S	A	U
T	H	A	N	E	■	S	C	A	N	■	S	A	W	S
O	S	L	E	R	■	H	A	M	S	■	A	Y	E	S

46

```
S P A N   O N I T   D O L L S
A L A I   G E S U N D H E I T
N A R C   R O O T Y T O O T Y
  N O O V E N U S E     N E E
M E N L O     T I T T L E S
I T B A N D S     S U E
M A U S   R A G E   M E S A S
E R R   H E A R T H S   E L I
S Y R I A   B E T A   B A I T
    A L T   A T L A R G E
  C O N T A C T   I R O N S
B A S   M A R S U P I U M
I N A N U P R O A R   S T E P
T A K E S A T U R N   T E N S
S L A T S   E T A S   A S T I
```

47

```
W I G   A S C O T S     P B S
I P A G L I A C C I   V I A L
D O N O T E N T E R   A L B A
E D G E   G O A L   I N O U T
    S P E E D L I M I T
  L E T O     C O L L A R
B O X   O N E I D A   L I P O
O U T O F O R D E R S I G N S
A I R Y   T R O W E L   H E Y
T E A S E R     E S T A
  S T E E P G R A D E
C A M E L   E L A N   N A S H
O M A R   R O A D C L O S E D
G E L S   I N C O H E R E N T
S N L   B Y E N O W   A T V
```

48

```
  I T S A L I E   N O I R
B R O W N A N D S E R V E
D U K E A N D D U C H E S S
P E R   T U E S   O R S
T A G T E A M S   C L U T C H
A L L W E T   B A D   E L I
S T E E R   T H A N   B I A S
  R I C E A N D B E A N S
D R A K E A N D J O S H
E O N S   M O J O   T A B L E
P L Y   A P R   C A V E A T
P E T A L S   A M A R E T T O
  H E P   E D O M   T I N
S M I T H A N D W E S S O N
P E N N A N D T E L L E R
A L G A   G O O D S O N
```

49

R	A	G	S		W	W	I				H	E	H	E
A	L	E	U	T	I	A	N		P	O	R	E	S	
P	A	T	R	I	C	K	S	T	E	W	A	R	T	
I	M	S		E	K	E		O	N	E	S	E	E	D
D	E	W	A	R	S		D	A	S			I	R	A
O	D	I	C			J	U	D	I	D	E	N	C	H
	A	T	T	U	N	E	D		E	R	R			
	H	U	G	O	W	E	A	V	I	N	G			
		A	G	R		T	H	E	B	E	A	N		
W	I	L	L	S	M	I	T	H			S	M	O	G
E	C	O			A	R	E		H	A	T	E	T	O
T	E	C	H	B	R	O		J	O	N		R	A	P
	C	H	A	R	A	C	T	E	R	A	C	T	O	R
	A	T	R	E	E		I	T	A	L	I	A	N	O
	P	E	E	R		X	E	S		A	G	E	S	

50

P	R	O	B	E		H	A	H	A		S	C	A	M
R	O	U	E	N		E	G	A	D		C	U	B	A
O	O	Z	E	D		R	A	N	S	C	A	R	E	D
	F	O	R	E	W	O	R	D		A	M	B	L	E
		N	A	A	N		P	E	R	P				
A	U	G	U	R	Y		D	I	C	T	I	O	N	
S	P	O	T	S		B	A	C	H	S		C	A	P
A	P	T	S		P	I	N	K	O		P	U	M	A
P	E	T		S	E	R	T	S		S	E	L	I	G
	D	I	C	T	A	T	E		S	C	R	I	B	E
		O	A	T	H		S	O	A	K				
E	A	R	L	Y		M	A	T	U	R	E	L	Y	
G	L	A	S	S	W	A	R	E		A	D	A	M	S
G	O	G	O		O	R	C	A		B	U	I	C	K
S	T	U	N		O	K	O	K		S	P	R	A	Y

51

H	O	R	D	E			C	U	R	R	E	N	C	Y
A	B	E	A	M		S	T	R	E	A	M	B	E	D
J	A	S	M	I	N	E	A	N	D	J	E	A	N	S
	D	A	N	G	E	R			D	A	R	T	S	
T	I	N		R	A	B	B	I			G	E	O	S
B	A	D	G	E	R	S	A	N	D	B	E	A	R	S
A	H	S	O			R	H	E	A		M	S	N	
		I	C	E	A	N	D	I	N	K				
P	S	I		A	L	S	O			A	U	D	I	
C	O	M	E	D	Y	A	N	D	C	R	I	M	E	S
T	W	I	X		P	E	C	O	S		P	M	S	
	S	T	A	T	S		U	N	V	O	T	E		
P	E	A	C	E	A	N	D	P	E	P	P	E	R	S
B	A	T	T	E	R	I	E	S		E	I	E	I	O
A	R	E	A	M	A	P	S			D	E	N	T	S

52

W	H	I	M		L	I	O	N		I	C	A	N	T
P	E	N	A		O	M	O	O		N	O	V	A	E
M	A	R	C	H	O	F	P	R	O	G	R	E	S	S
	R	E	A	R			S	E	X		D	R	A	T
S	I	T		W	E	B	B		E	X	P	O		
K	O	H	L	S		L	I	M	N		A	N	G	E	R
E	D	I	E		D	E	L	I		L	A	B	I	L	E
W	I	N	T	E	R	W	O	N	D	E	R	L	A	N	D
E	D	G	I	L	Y		X	I	I	I		E	N	I	D
R	E	S	T	S		L	I	M	B		B	U	T	N	O
			S	A	T	E		A	S	T	I		P	O	T
T	A	I	L		A	T	L			O	K	R	A		
S	P	R	I	N	G	H	A	S	S	P	R	U	N	G
A	S	A	D	A		A	L	A	I		A	N	D	Y
R	E	N	E	W		L	A	M	B		M	E	A	N

53

O	W	L	E	T		I	D	A		S	C	A	L	P
C	H	I	N	M	U	S	I	C		L	U	C	I	A
H	A	N	G	E	H	I	G	H		O	T	T	E	R
E	T	E		N	O	T			M	T	C	O	O	K
R	A	D			H	O	O	K	E	H	O	R	N	S
	T	A	D	A		K	A	O	S					
B	O	N	A	M	I		T	O	M	B		X	C	I
R	O	C	K	E	S	O	C	K	E	R	O	B	O	T
A	L	E		N	O	V	A		R	U	N	O	N	S
			M	I	K	E		T	E	X	T			
K	N	O	C	K	E	D	E	A	D		G	I	G	
R	E	I	N	E	R		T	I	M		A	N	Y	
A	L	L	O	Y		S	T	I	C	K	E	M	U	P
F	L	U	T	E		P	I	N	E	T	R	E	E	S
T	Y	P	E	D		F	O	G		S	A	S	S	Y

54

D	R	O	S	S		A	C	T	S		A	S	S	A	D
A	I	S	L	E		P	L	O	W		U	T	E	R	O
T	A	C	I	T		H	O	M	E		R	U	L	E	R
E	T	A	T	S		I	D	E	A		I	B	E	A	M
D	A	R		I	T	D		T	N	G		S	S	S	
			U	N	O				O	A	F				
T	W	O	S		I	N	M	O	S	T		C	B	G	B
O	H	N	O		L	E	A	G	U	E		C	A	R	E
M	A	E		S	E	A	C	R	E	S	T		R	A	E
S	T	A	S	H		T	H	E	Y		S	A	T	Y	R
	A	L	L	A	N					V	A	L	E	S	
O	B	L	I	Q	U	E	R	E	F	E	R	E	N	C	E
R	O	T	C		K	R	O	N	E	R		P	D	A	S
B	R	I	E		E	T	U	D	E	S		P	E	L	T
S	E	E	D		S	E	E	S	T	O		O	D	E	D

55

```
L A I D A W A Y ■ B A R C A R
A L T E R E G O ■ E X H A L E
M A I N M E N U ■ S E E F I T
A S S ■ ■ E D I T ■ S E A R
■ ■ S H O W I N ■ G U S S Y
L A P T O P ■ D U K E S ■
A C H E B E ■ W R I T ■ A M P
C H E W O N T ■ E M O N G E R
Y E W ■ B L O C ■ O N A U T O
■ ■ S A Y A H ■ N I N E A M
S H R U G ■ D E S O T O ■
H O O D ■ ■ M Y T H ■ M A D
I M G O N E ■ J A R L O O S E
P E E K I N ■ O L D L A T I N
S Y R U P S ■ B L A C K H A T
```

56

```
T R I P ■ C L O T H ■ A V A
R A V E ■ D O N H O ■ T S A R
I C A N T S L E E P A W I N K
B E N T O ■ I B C ■ C A F
E R A ■ K I T C H E N S I N
■ V E N A ■ A X E ■ C A P
■ F R A N C ■ E M T ■ J A D E
P O U R ■ H O T P I ■ A R E A
A R M Y ■ A K A ■ N E W E R
C U R ■ B O A ■ A C T S
■ M A K E S Y O U T H ■ P D T
■ I R E ■ D V D ■ A L L A Y
D I S A P P E A R I N G I N K
D R I B ■ E A T E N ■ B E N E
S A N ■ G R E Y S ■ T S O S
```

57

```
M A D D A S H ■ A T T R A C T
A R E O L A E ■ S A O I R S E
V I C T O R / V I C T O R I A
■ T E A S E D O U T ■
R E F I S ■ H I E ■ P A S T S
E T R E ■ T E N S E ■ C L I P
T H O R P E ■ T A T A M I
I N S ■ R E D F L A G ■ S E C
N I T ■ I S R A E L I ■ H R E
A C / D C ■ R C A ■ L O E S S
■ N E E ■ O E D ■ E R R
S K I M ■ A M / F M ■ A F A R
X O X O ■ M A O R I ■ N I L E
S L O T ■ I N F E R ■ G L U M
W A N E ■ N O F E E ■ E M M Y
```

58

```
C L O M P   ▓ N I G H ▓ C A S H
A U D I S   ▓ O R E O ▓ A B U T
R A I N Y   ▓ P A T T Y M E L T
▓ U N I C O R N S T A R T U P
▓ ▓ ▓ H B O ▓ ▓ A M Y ▓ ▓ ▓
Z O M B I E B A N K S ▓ H I P
I S A A C ▓ ▓ C U E ▓ M O N A
P A R R ▓ S H U N S ▓ E W A N
I K I D ▓ E A T ▓ ▓ A I S L E
T A O ▓ P A T E N T T R O L L
▓ ▓ B A R ▓ ▓ O A T ▓ ▓ ▓
F I N A N C I A L M Y T H S
O V E R S H A R E ▓ G H A N A
C A I N ▓ E G G S ▓ E R R O R
I N N S ▓ R O O S ▓ N U D G E
```

59

```
I C A N ▓ A B E S ▓ D A W G S
N O N O ▓ S E R E ▓ O C H O A
F R O M W H E R E I S T A N D
I R I S H ▓ F O P S ▓ S T E T
D I N G O ▓ C R E E P ▓ A B A
E D T ▓ A D A ▓ D E C I M A L
L A S S ▓ E K E ▓ B S I D E
▓ ▓ ▓ P O W E R L E S S ▓ ▓
S H A F T ▓ A I L ▓ O P R Y
P E R S I S T ▓ Z I P ▓ R A E
O R R ▓ S K O A L ▓ I P O D S
N O I R ▓ Y A L E ▓ P U P I L
G I V E M E S O M E S P A C E
E N A C T ▓ T H O R ▓ A N A T
D E L T A ▓ S A N S ▓ E E L S
```

60

```
E R R ▓ C A B O ▓ S E D A N
G O E S A L L I N ▓ T U X E D O
G I F T G U I D E ▓ I C E S I N
▓ ▓ R A B I E S V A C C I N E
I M O U T ▓ ▓ E I R E ▓ ▓ ▓
N O R T H W E S T P A S S A G E
T O W ▓ A S A P ▓ ▓ S A M O A
A S H E ▓ U R A N U S ▓ G A L S
C H A R O ▓ ▓ O N I T ▓ Z E E
T U T A N K H A M E N S T O M B
▓ ▓ S O U L ▓ ▓ E E N S Y ▓
S E A R C H R E S U L T S ▓ ▓
P A R C E L ▓ R E M A S T E R S
A V I A N S ▓ T E N N E S S E E
T E A S E ▓ S M O G ▓ ▓ P O X
```

61

```
B O A S  ▪  B Y O B ▪ H E R A
A R N E ▪  S A U N A ▪ O N E G
(YOU)C A N T T A K E I T W I T H
▪ C A R A ▪ S A L A ▪ G I A
T W O T E R M ▪ (BOND)J A M E S
K A N E ▪ L O T T ▪ N A S T
O L D ▪ Y E S W E C A N ▪
▪ (DO)A S I S A Y N O T A S I
▪ O N S I L E N T ▪ N A P
K O P F ▪ C A T E ▪ C A G E
(NO)M E A N S ▪ S H O O K O N
B E N ▪ A L V A ▪ E A V E
B A C K T O S Q U A R E O N E
E R I E ▪ G O U R D ▪ R I G A
D A L Y ▪ S P A N ▪ S L O T
```

62

```
R E B U S ▪ A Q A B A ▪ I C E
A R O S E ▪ M U N I S ▪ N O G
W O N O N P O I N T S ▪ A L E
B I N ▪ T A C T ▪ M O U N D S
A C E S ▪ T O O D A R N H O T
R A T E D R ▪ O P T I O N S
▪ Q U O T A S ▪ V U E
▪ D O U B L E H E A D E R S
▪ O V O ▪ S A D D E R
A G E I S T S ▪ W E S S O N
F O R A C H A N G E ▪ E T N A
F O C S L E ▪ F U E L ▪ E R G
I D O ▪ A T E L I K E A P I G
R E A ▪ S O R E S ▪ T W I C E
M R T ▪ S P A R E ▪ O W N E D
```

63

```
B O S S Y ▪ D I O R ▪ H A M
Y A H O O ▪ I R A E ▪ C A S E
E T H Y L ▪ D A H L ▪ A V I A
▪ B A R O Q U E B R E A D
A R D E N T ▪ A L P I N E
P A R A D E F O R R A I N ▪
A M A N A ▪ I W O N T ▪ S I C
R E F S ▪ M E N U S ▪ H T M L
T N T ▪ P E R E S ▪ H O O H A
▪ C O L L I D E B A R R O W
A S H P I T ▪ O N S E T S
T H O R E A U S H A D E ▪
L E I A ▪ W O K E ▪ O C H E R
A R C H ▪ A F E W ▪ F A U V E
S E E ▪ Y A W N ▪ F R E E D
```

64

```
R O T H   M O S S Y     J A W S
A C R E   A N I M E S   A V O W
S T A L E C E R E A L   M A K E
C A D E T S     A R I A   T E A
A G E N T   B U R N T T O A S T
L O O   A E O N     S O R T S
  N F L   L A M B   P E P
    F I X B R E A K F A S T
    B R A   T G I F   Y U P
A P N E A     E T T U   N A P
M E A L Y A P P L E   S L A T E
I R E   S L U R   H E I F E R
G U N N   S P O I L E D M I L K
A S A P   O I N K E R   I S L E
S E E R   L E E D S   T H A D
```

65

```
C A B B A G E     G A S B A G
O V O I D A L     O F N O T E
P A N D E M I C   S T A B L E
I N T O N E   A S P E R
E T O N   B U T T E R F L Y
S I N   C O S E L L   O E D
    P A Y E R   S T E N O S
U B E R S   S P A   R I G H T
G A T E A U   I C E I N
G N C   S A L A A M   D J S
  C H R Y S A L I S   F R A T
    H A T H A   E C L A I R
A R G Y L E   R E D E A G L E
R O O M I E   P I N K O E S
S E A E E L   I N T E N D S
```

66

```
D E C L A R E     S W I P E S
E M A I L I N G   T E R E S A
F O R B I D D E N P L A N E T
A T A R I   R E A C T
M E T A   S H E S T H E M A N
E S S   O U I     E R A
  M A S T E R   O M I T S
W E S T S I D E S T O R Y
I W I S H   T O M A T O
L I N   I M O   M A Y
K I S S M E K A T E   T I R E
  A E S O P   D I S C S
S H A K E S P E A R E P L A Y
T A L E S E   S T A M P E D E
U N I S E X   M Y S I D E S
```

67

W	I	T	C	H	H	U	N	T	■	A	G	A	S	P
E	M	E	R	G	E	N	C	Y	■	R	U	N	T	O
E	S	T	A	T	E	C	A	R	■	T	A	T	A	S
D	E	R	N	■	D	A	R	E	D	E	V	I	L	S
S	T	A	N	C	E	S	■	A	M	A	L	I	E	■
■	I	E	D	■	A	R	T	I	S	A	N	S	■	■
S	T	E	E	L	■	J	I	V	E	S	■	B	I	S
E	R	A	S	■	B	O	D	E	D	■	B	O	S	E
X	E	R	■	F	A	K	E	R	■	H	U	R	T	S
C	A	T	S	E	Y	E	S	■	G	O	D	■	■	■
A	D	H	E	R	E	■	■	D	O	G	S	P	A	S
P	E	T	E	R	R	O	G	E	T	■	E	L	S	E
A	D	O	S	E	■	N	I	C	H	O	L	A	S	I
D	O	N	A	T	■	E	L	C	A	P	I	T	A	N
E	N	E	W	S	■	B	L	A	M	E	G	A	M	E

68

H	A	L	L	P	A	S	S	■	■	G	A	P	P	Y
O	L	I	G	A	R	C	H	■	S	O	I	R	E	E
P	I	B	B	X	T	R	A	■	P	A	N	E	R	A
I	C	E	T	■	S	O	B	S	I	S	T	E	R	S
S	E	R	R	A	■	D	B	A	C	K	■	N	Y	T
■	F	A	I	R	S	■	A	T	E	A	T	■	■	■
N	A	T	G	E	O	■	T	U	R	N	R	I	P	E
E	Y	E	H	A	N	D	■	P	A	Y	A	F	E	E
W	E	S	T	C	O	R	K	■	C	O	V	E	N	S
■	■	■	S	O	F	I	A	■	K	N	E	E	S	■
O	T	B	■	D	A	N	Z	A	■	E	L	L	I	E
C	O	O	K	E	D	K	A	L	E	■	B	L	O	W
T	R	A	U	M	A	■	K	E	T	E	L	O	N	E
A	I	R	D	A	M	■	H	U	N	G	O	V	E	R
D	I	D	U	P	■	■	S	T	A	G	G	E	R	S

69

I	I	N	S	I	S	T	■	C	O	L	L	A	T	E
S	T	E	A	M	E	R	■	A	V	I	A	T	O	R
L	E	A	S	E	T	O	■	R	O	O	T	F	O	R
E	M	P	H	A	S	I	S	M	I	N	E	■	■	■
■	A	N	A	■	Q	E	D	■	C	A	B	S	■	■
Z	A	N	Y	■	G	A	U	L	■	L	A	P	E	L
A	P	E	■	B	O	L	A	■	L	O	L	I	T	A
P	O	R	T	R	A	I	T	G	A	L	L	E	R	Y
P	L	U	R	A	L	■	J	A	Z	Z	■	C	U	E
E	L	D	O	N	■	R	U	B	Y	■	F	E	E	D
R	O	A	M	■	J	A	M	■	B	O	O	■	■	■
■	■	■	B	O	O	K	P	R	O	P	O	S	A	L
L	E	M	O	N	D	E	■	O	N	A	D	A	T	E
S	C	E	N	E	I	I	■	M	E	R	I	N	O	S
T	O	H	E	L	E	N	■	E	S	T	E	E	M	S

70

```
O R G A N . . O C T A L . A M O
K O E N I G . W H A T A T R I P
S A N C H O . E A T A T H O M E
O N E H A L F . R E D E E M E R
. S T O O D U P . . A S A D A .
. . . E T R E . L P S . . . .
L I N M A N U E L M I R A N D A
I N A L L P R O B A B I L I T Y
Z O M B I E A P O C A L Y P S E
. . D E N . S W A T . . . . .
C H U R N . . S W I F F E R .
R A R A A V I S . S O L O C U P
A S I F T O S A Y . N I C O L E
S T A T E L I N E . S E A L E R
H E H . D E S K S . . D L I S T
```

71

```
T R O I . A B U T . D A N T E
B O X C A M E R A . S P E A R
S P E E D B A L L . T H A T S
P E N T H O U S E S U I T E .
. . R O Y . . A D D A M S
A F L A C . G A B L E . S O Y
C L A Y . N E M E A N . A D D
E A T . C O L B E R T . P E N
T M I . O D D I T Y . D I R E
I B N . R E S T S . S U N N Y
C O L A D A . . G P S . .
. Y O G U R T S M O O T H I E
C A V E R . I N A M O R A T A
O N E N O . P I X E L A T E D
S T R A Y . S T I R . G E M S
```

72

```
B M X . G O T M E . C H A S M
B O D Y S P R A Y . R A N T S
Q U I E T T I M E . I D T A G
S E N O R I T A S . P A S T .
. . . M I C E . T R E F O I L
A S I A N S . P R E S E N C E
C H A N G . F O A L . W A L T
C O M . S E A L I O N . L I T
O P A L . T R O N . B O O N E
S A M A D A M S . D A N G E R
T H E B E S T . V E G A . .
. O R C A . E R I C A J O N G
E L I O T . A U T O M A K E R
M I C A H . M B A D E G R E E
S C A T S . S E L E S . A D S
```

73

D	N	A	L	A	B	S		B	J	N	O	V	A	K
R	O	S	E	C	U	T		Y	O	U	L	O	S	E
O	X	I	D	A	T	E		L	U	D	D	I	T	E
O	Z	S		I	N	E	X	I	L	E		D	A	B
P	E	A	S		O	P	I	N	E		G	I	R	L
E	M	I	T	S		L	I	E		M	O	N	T	E
D	A	D	J	O	K	E		S	W	A	G	G	E	R
		O	D	E				B	R	R				
M	A	C	H	O	N	E		C	A	K	E	M	I	X
O	M	A	N	I		A	B	U		S	E	E	M	S
N	I	P	S		S	T	I	E	S		N	A	P	A
A	R	T		B	A	I	T	C	A	R		N	I	N
R	I	C	O	A	C	T		A	D	A	P	T	E	D
C	T	H	U	L	H	U		R	I	S	O	T	T	O
H	E	A	T	M	A	P		D	E	P	L	O	Y	S

74

F	I	F	T	H	E	S	T	A	T	E		A	H	S
I	R	A	R	O	L	L	O	V	E	R		R	E	A
R	U	M	O	R	M	O	N	G	E	R		G	A	D
S	L	E	D	S		G	I	A	N		R	E	D	S
T	E	D			P	A	C	S		M	E	N	L	O
			A	S	I	N			E	A	S	T	O	N
		B	I	N	G	E	W	A	T	C	H	I	N	G
	P	A	R	O	L	E	H	E	A	R	I	N	G	
S	L	I	P	P	E	R	Y	S	L	O	P	E		
C	O	L	L	E	T			T	I	N	S			
I	D	E	A	S		M	A	H	I		M	S	G	
E	D	D	Y		R	O	M	E		P	R	O	W	L
N	E	O		P	I	R	A	T	E	R	A	D	I	O
C	R	U		C	A	N	T	I	L	E	V	E	R	S
E	S	T		B	A	S	I	C	S	K	I	L	L	S

75

R	M	S		W	A	S	A	B	I		A	B	C	S
O	A	T		I	P	C	R	E	S	S	F	I	L	E
C	U	M		C	O	U	G	H	B	U	T	T	O	N
K	N	O	C	K		B	O	O	N	E		E	S	T
F	A	R	O		M	A	N	N		T	I	M	E	R
A	K	I	N		A	S	N	E	R		F	E	T	A
N	E	T	T	E	R		E	S	S	A	Y			
S	A	Z	E	R	A	C		T	V	H	O	S	T	S
			S	M	U	R	F		P	A	U	L	I	V
S	A	R	S		D	I	O	D	E		C	O	D	E
C	L	E	A	T		T	R	O	D		A	T	I	T
U	G	G		O	V	I	T	Z		I	N	T	E	L
F	O	I	A	R	E	Q	U	E	S	T		I	D	A
F	R	O	N	T	R	U	N	N	E	R		N	U	N
S	E	N	D		Y	E	A	S	T	Y		G	P	A

76

P	O	S	T	E	R	I	Z	E	■	L	A	S	T	S
E	S	C	A	P	E	P	O	D	■	A	R	H	A	T
W	H	A	T	S	M	O	R	E	■	Z	A	I	R	E
S	A	N	T	O	■	■	A	R	M	Y	B	R	A	T
■	■	O	M	A	R	■	O	B	S	E	S	S	■	■
C	A	M	O	■	G	O	S	O	L	O	■			
O	F	F	I	C	E	M	A	X	■	N	E	A	T	O
S	T	A	S	H	■	A	L	I	■	E	X	C	O	P
T	A	S	T	E	■	N	U	D	E	S	C	E	N	E
■	■	■	E	R	O	D	E	D	■	U	S	E	D	■
L	A	O	T	Z	U	■	■	S	U	S	S	■		
I	T	S	A	W	R	A	P	■	■	C	E	A	S	E
L	E	A	S	H	■	S	A	Y	S	A	Y	S	A	Y
T	A	K	E	I	■	A	R	I	S	T	O	T	L	E
S	T	A	R	Z	■	P	A	N	T	S	U	I	T	S

77

R	A	T	P	A	C	K	■	■	N	B	A	J	A	M
E	U	R	A	S	I	A	N	■	Y	E	S	I	D	O
A	B	U	D	H	A	B	I	■	S	E	W	N	O	N
P	A	I	R	■	O	L	G	A	■	N	A	G	A	T
E	D	S	E	L	■	O	H	M	S	■	N	O	N	A
R	E	M	■	E	X	O	T	I	C	A	■	I	N	N
■	■	H	A	R	E	M	■	R	U	S	S	I	A	■
■	O	N	E	D	A	Y	A	T	A	T	I	M	E	■
G	R	O	M	I	T	■	R	A	P	I	D	■		
A	D	S	■	N	E	M	E	S	E	S	■	P	A	C
N	E	L	L	■	D	A	F	T	■	M	A	R	S	H
G	R	O	A	N	■	S	U	E	Z	■	R	O	S	A
S	O	U	P	E	D	■	E	B	E	N	E	Z	E	R
T	U	C	S	O	N	■	L	U	K	E	W	A	R	M
A	T	H	E	N	A	■	D	E	T	E	C	T	S	

78

G	A	S	T	A	P	■	■	R	A	T	E	D	G
O	N	L	I	N	E	■	B	E	D	E	L	I	A
F	I	E	S	T	A	■	H	A	D	A	L	I	S	P
O	M	E	N	S	■	F	I	R	E	P	L	A	C	E
R	A	P	T	■	B	I	G	B	A	T	S	■		
A	N	A	■	E	X	H	A	L	E	■	P	O	I
S	I	P	S	■	G	E	A	R	T	R	A	I	N	S
P	A	N	I	C	■	D	N	A	■	S	T	E	E	L
I	C	E	C	A	P	A	D	E	S	■	E	R	M	A
N	S	A	■	D	E	S	A	D	E	■	C	A	N	
■	■	G	E	T	S	W	E	T	■	T	E	N	D	
O	R	S	O	N	B	E	A	N	■	J	U	D	A	H
H	O	S	T	C	I	T	Y	■	B	O	L	E	R	O
H	U	N	T	E	R	S	■	U	V	L	A	M	P	
I	T	S	O	D	D	■	B	E	E	R	Y	S		

79

```
C H I P   E A S Y     K E P T
L E N O   F R E E   H I L L Y
A M A N   F R E S H E N S U P
S O N D H E I M   E N G A G E
S P Y   E T D   U R S A
C H E V R E   F L O O R S I T
L I V E R   M A C I N T O S H
O L E G   B I D E N   H U M E
W I N E M A K E R   T U N E R
N A T T E R E D   G I R D L E
    A S I S   B A M   B L T
C H A R O N   J E R E M I A H
L I V I N G D E A D   E T R E
A L I A S   I D L E   R E A R
M O A N   M I E N   E S T E
```

80

```
M A L L C O P   C A P S T A N
E T A I L E R   A B A L O N E
D O T T E D I   R E W O R D S
E N E R O   O D E   N O T I T
V E R E   C R I E D   P O R E
A G O   S H E E R E D   N O G
C O N S T A N T C R A V I N G
      T A N G E R I N E
A L T E R N A T I V E R O C K
I O U   R E G I M E S   V O N
R U M S   L E C I D   R E N E
B E B O P   M S N   P E R V S
A L L R I S E   A D H E R E S
S L E E P I N   L E I S U R E
E A R N E S T   S I L E N T T
```

81

```
M A L T A   E P S     F T L B
A T E O F   M O O R   R O O M
S T A R R   P O L I C E B O X
K I S S O N T H E C H E E K
  C H I P P Y   H A Z E S
    O U R   S C E N E X I V
D J I N N   O A R S   R A N I
I A N   K I B B U T Z   C O D
E N I D   N I L E   A E T N A
S E T A D A T E   H M M
  T I R E S   F I B B E R
  M A K E U P T U T O R I A L
G O L D M I N E R   N A D J A
U C L A   T I L L   I C E I N
S K Y Y   N E S   S E R V E
```

82

```
A L E R T ■ C H I N A S H O P
G O P E R ■ L E M O N L I M E
E V I T A ■ E M P T Y E Y E S
R E C I D I V I S M ■ D A L E
A B I L E N E ■ ■ E A G L E T
N O S E S P R A Y ■ D E L T A
G A T S ■ A D H E R E S ■ ■ ■
E T S ■ T R I E S O N ■ M U M
■ ■ L I T C R I T ■ R E N O
A D D E R ■ K O N A C O A S T
N O O S E S ■ ■ D R A G N E T
G M O S ■ K A T E Y S A G A L
L I V E S A L I E ■ S I E T E
O N E P U T T E D ■ I N N E R
S I R S P E E D Y ■ S E E D S
```

83

```
M A M A B I R D ■ T U R N I P
O S O L E M I O ■ I C H E C K
W E L L D A M N ■ G L O V E S
S A D E ■ F A T H E A D E D ■
■ R C A ■ W A R ■ A R C O
■ P A G A N ■ A R M S ■ F O B
A L L I N ■ Z I P O N ■ A F I
W E L C O M E T O M Y L I F E
M A O ■ N O R U N ■ D A L E S
A S S ■ S L O P ■ D E N S E
N E A P ■ A T F ■ O R D
■ S U R F S H O P S ■ L A C E
A T R O I S ■ R E A R A X L E
M O U S S E ■ M E G A D E A L
U P S E T S ■ E N E M Y S P Y
```

84

```
S T N A D E R ■ S D A P S O S
I H A V E T O ■ B A Y L E A F
T A W O R H T ■ E M N O S T I
O N E W A Y S T R E E T S ■
■ E L A Y ■ S A P S
I N S E T ■ R O B O ■ T H O
N A M T ■ L L A N I G N I O G
A R O U S A L ■ D R E A M E R
S N O I T C E R I D ■ T E B A
A I R ■ M E T A ■ M O D E L
D A E B ■ N A L E ■
■ T O T A L G R I D L O C K
S D A O R N I ■ O T N I G O L
H O T Z O N E ■ G R A N O L A
O N S E T O V ■ A E T E G A S
```

85

H	E	L	I	C	O	P	T	E	R	P	A	R	E	N	T
A	R	U	N	F	O	R	O	N	E	S	M	O	N	E	Y
S	O	N	I	C	D	E	P	T	H	F	I	N	D	E	R
P	S	A	T		L	E	E	R	Y		D	O	D	O	
		R	I	P	E	N			D	A	Z	E			
S	C	R	A	P	S		M	E	R	C	I	L	E	S	S
C	L	O	T	S		L	E	V	A	N	T		Z	E	E
R	A	V	E		D	E	L	E	T	E		S	P	O	T
E	R	E		S	E	V	E	R	E		S	T	A	U	B
W	A	R	B	A	B	I	E	S		M	E	A	S	L	Y
		R	O	S	A			G	E	A	R	S			
E	S	M	E		T	R	O	U	T		E	L	M	O	
T	H	A	T	S	W	H	A	T	S	H	E	S	A	I	D
D	O	Y	O	U	W	A	N	T	T	O	D	A	N	C	E
S	T	A	N	D	I	N	G	O	O	D	S	T	E	A	D

86

C	O	F	F	E	E	M	A	T	E		T	O	J	O
O	N	I	O	N	B	A	G	E	L		U	P	O	N
B	E	E	R	G	A	R	I	T	A		N	E	V	E
R	A	N	K	I	N		T	A	N	Z	A	N	I	A
A	L	D	E	N		T	A	N	D	E	M	S		
			D	E	P	U	T	Y		N	E	W	E	L
R	I	M		N	I	N	E		P	O	L	I	T	E
I	R	E	F	U	S	E		L	O	S	T	D	O	G
P	A	N	A	M	A		D	O	U	P		E	N	O
S	Q	U	I	B		R	U	B	R	A	W			
		P	R	E	C	E	S	S		R	I	C	H	E
N	B	A	D	R	A	F	T		M	A	N	N	E	R
Y	O	G	I		C	O	P	I	E	D	D	O	W	N
A	L	E	C		T	R	A	M	R	O	U	T	E	S
H	O	S	E		I	M	N	O	E	X	P	E	R	T

87

C	U	S	S	E	R			A	D	J	U	S	T
U	N	M	I	X	E	D		C	R	A	N	I	A
S	T	O	R	E	S	U	P		Q	U	I	N	N	S
T	A	K	E	M	O	R	E		U	M	L	A	U	T
O	P	E	N	P	L	A	N		I	R	A	I	S	E
M	E	S	S	T	E	N	T		R	O	B	L	E	S
				G	A	Z	E	L	L	E	S	
		H	O	W	S	O		I	D	L	E	D	
	H	A	V	E	A	S	I	P					
B	O	R	E	A	L		M	P	E	G	F	I	L	E
S	P	A	R	S	E		S	E	A	R	A	V	E	N
T	E	N	D	E	D		A	R	R	E	S	T	E	D
A	N	G	O	L	A		D	E	N	A	T	U	R	E
R	O	U	S	E	Y			D	I	V	E	B	A	R
S	T	E	E	D	S			T	E	N	E	T	S	

88

```
S O D A C A N S █ C A M E B Y
E C O L A B E L █ U R A N I A
A T T E N D T O █ P E S T E R
M I C R O U S B █ O N H O L D
A L O T █ C U B S F A N █ █
N E D █ S T R E E T █ O M A R
█ █ O A K █ F R E E S T Y L E
A N T L E R █ █ A L E T A P
C O U L D I T B E █ A S H █
A N K A █ O H E N R Y █ B B S
█ B U T A L S O · S U C H
S O L O N G A L I P A S H A
C R E A T E B A D A C T O R
A Z A R I A O V E R H E R E
B O R D E R █ R E D C A R D S
```

89

```
G U A R █ R I N D █ F R A T
O N S A L E N O W █ G R E C O
A S I F I C A R E █ R E T R Y
T H A T S A L I E █ A E R O S
S Y N █ P S A █ B A D C O P █
█ █ L E T T S █ P S Y C H O
A S F A R █ H I D E █ C O O P
S C A M █ R E L A X █ L O B E
E R T E █ A R T Y █ D E L E D
S A F E S T █ S T A R S █
█ P I X I E S █ R E Y █ B R A
T I N C T █ P H A R M A R E P
A R G U E █ A U D I O T A P E
L O E S S █ S L E E P O V E R
I N R E █ M A R S █ P O L Y
```

90

```
I P A S S █ T A P E █ P D A
M O N A E █ I M A X █ B R U N
D I D J A █ M O T O R B I K E
O S H A █ T B S █ I B E A M
W O O K I E E █ L P S █ S K I
N N W █ N A R C O L E P T I C
█ █ P A B L O C A S A L S █
█ D E C L A R A T O R Y █
█ D A R L E N E L O V E █
D O N E A N D D O N E █ L A S
R T E █ I D S · F I R E A X E
O C C U R █ A F C █ S T I X
P O O P E M O J I █ A T I L T
I M O N █ G U A C █ M E N L O
T S K █ M I R E █ T E X A N
```

91

S	T	A	R	S	H	I	P	S	■	S	O	N	I	A
C	H	I	C	K	A	S	A	W	■	A	X	O	N	S
R	E	L	A	Y	R	A	C	E	■	M	E	S	S	I
U	T	E	■	■	D	W	E	E	B	■	N	E	T	S
B	A	D	P	R	■	■	T	A	M	■	S	E	A	■
■	■	R	I	M	■	F	E	T	A	■	T	R	I	■
■	T	O	B	E	C	O	N	T	I	N	U	E	D	■
W	H	A	T	S	H	O	U	L	D	I	D	O	■	■
C	H	E	M	I	C	A	L	P	E	E	L	S	■	■
R	E	M	■	P	A	N	S	■	S	N	L	■	■	■
E	R	A	■	S	L	C	■	■	S	A	L	E	M	■
S	E	T	H	■	S	E	V	E	N	■	O	V	A	■
T	A	R	O	T	■	D	A	T	A	M	I	N	E	R
E	M	I	L	E	■	I	N	A	M	O	M	E	N	T
D	I	X	I	E	■	T	E	L	E	P	O	R	T	S

92

N	E	S	T	C	E	P	A	S	■	A	M	P	A	S
A	L	P	H	A	M	A	L	E	■	L	A	R	C	H
M	A	U	I	W	O	W	I	E	■	A	G	I	T	A
A	I	R	S	■	J	A	G	■	A	N	I	M	A	L
T	N	T	■	H	I	T	H	E	R	■	C	E	L	L
H	E	S	S	E	■	■	T	A	C	O	■	R	O	W
■	■	■	C	A	L	I	■	T	A	N	L	I	N	E
■	C	L	O	R	O	X	■	E	N	R	O	B	E	■
C	H	I	T	O	W	N	■	N	E	A	R	■	■	■
H	U	M	■	F	R	A	T	■	■	M	E	R	C	H
I	G	O	R	■	E	Y	E	C	U	P	■	A	H	A
C	A	R	A	T	S	■	J	O	N	■	E	T	A	L
A	L	I	V	E	■	C	A	N	D	Y	G	I	R	L
N	U	D	E	S	■	I	N	D	I	E	G	O	G	O
A	G	E	N	T	■	G	O	O	D	A	S	N	E	W

93

D	R	Y	■	L	O	O	F	A	■	A	S	A	N	A
J	U	M	B	O	T	R	O	N	■	C	A	B	O	T
E	S	C	A	P	E	K	E	Y	■	E	R	N	I	E
D	E	A	N	S	L	I	S	T	■	T	O	E	S	■
■	■	■	K	I	L	N	■	A	V	E	N	G	E	D
M	A	D	E	D	O	■	S	K	I	N	G	A	M	E
E	V	A	D	E	■	B	L	E	D	■	S	T	A	T
N	E	T	■	D	E	L	I	R	I	A	■	I	K	E
A	R	I	A	■	G	U	M	S	■	L	A	V	E	R
C	A	N	T	L	O	S	E	■	W	A	D	E	R	S
E	G	G	H	A	S	H	■	P	E	N	S	■	■	■
■	E	P	I	C	■	P	O	R	T	H	O	L	E	S
B	J	O	R	K	■	I	M	O	N	A	R	O	L	L
M	O	O	S	E	■	N	A	V	A	L	B	A	S	E
W	E	L	T	Y	■	K	N	O	P	E	■	F	E	W